Cyprus, the Pyramids and the Holy Land
2nd Edition

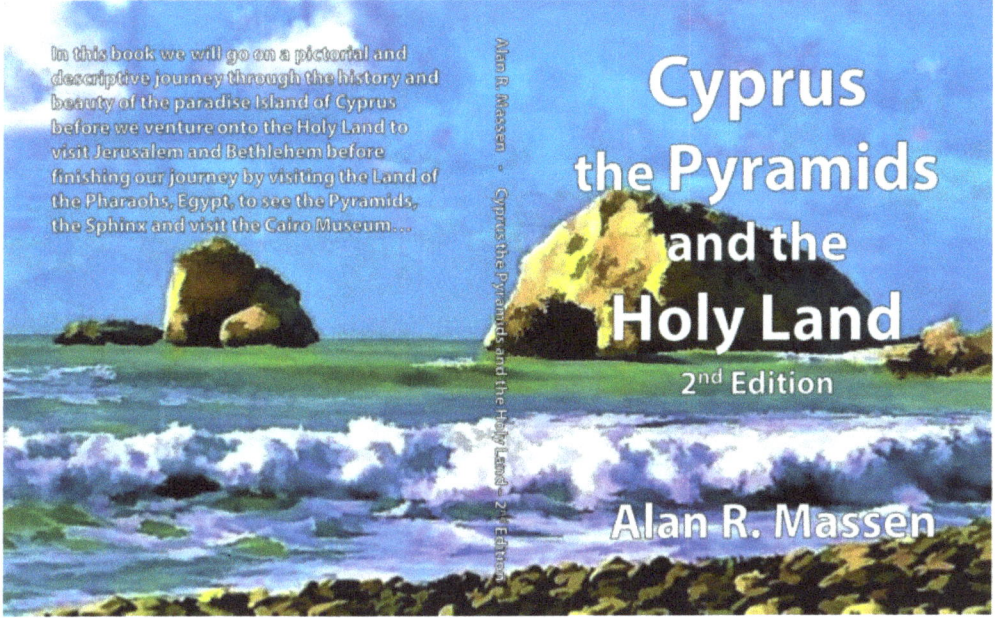

This book is a pictorial and descriptive journey through the history and beauty of the paradise island of Cyprus. We then venture onto the Holy Land to visit Jerusalem and Bethlehem before finishing our journey in the land of the Pharaohs, Egypt, to visit the Pyramids, the Sphinx and the City of Cairo Museum.

by Norfolk Watercolour Artist - Alan R. Massen
Published in Great Britain by Rainbow Publications UK

First Published in 2018 by Rainbow Publications UK
2nd Edition Published in 2019 by Rainbow Publications UK

Copyright © 2019 Alan R. Massen

The moral right of Alan R. Massen to be identified as the author of this work has been asserted in accordance with the UK Copyright, Designs and Patents Act of 1988. All rights reserved.

No part of this book may be reproduced, or stored in a retrieval system, or transmitted in any form or by any means, electronic, mechanical, photocopying, recording, or otherwise, without the prior written permission of both the author and the above publisher of this book All imagery and illustrations

© Alan R. Massen

Neither the publisher nor the author can accept liability for the use of any of the materials, methods or information recommended in this book or for any consequences arising out of their use, nor can they be held responsible for any errors or omissions that may be found in the text or may occur at a future date as a result of changes in rules, laws or equipment All manufacturers, sellers, product names and services identified in this book are used in editorial fashion and for the benefit of such companies with no intention of any infringement of trademarks. No such use or the use of any trade name is intended to convey endorsement or other affiliation with this book

Paperback Edition ISBN 978-0-9935591-7-4
Typeset in Minion Pro
Published in Great Britain by Rainbow Publications UK

About the Author

Alan was born in the city of Norwich in the county of Norfolk, England in November 1949. When Alan was still a teenager he started painting whilst attending art classes in Norwich. In his mid-teens he had two paintings accepted for a National Art Exhibition held in London and other major UK cities. Alan spent most of his working life as a professional Health and Safety Advisor and rarely picked up a paint brush until Alan, his wife Susie and daughter Ginny (his other daughter Mandy is married and lives with her husband Adrian in Sheffield) moved out of the city of Norwich into the countryside in 1993. They moved to a little village called East Lexham in the heart of Norfolk. The village was very peaceful and pretty. This helped inspire Alan to take up watercolour painting once again. In 2004 they moved to another small West Norfolk village near Downham Market where they still live today. In 2008 Alan had to retire due to ill health (bad knees) and whilst he still painted regularly he began to spend more and more time gardening. In 2013 his wife Susie suggested that he kept a gardening diary to record his adventures in the garden and capture the changing seasons, animals, birds and the successes and failures of being a gardener he encountered. By the following year Susie suggested that he should write a book from his diary and include illustrations of both the garden and his artwork.

In 2014 Alan's first book was published by Creative Gateway called **"Retiring to the Garden – Year One".** This proved such a success that Alan decided to follow this up with his second book called **"Retiring into a Rainbow"** featuring his watercolour paintings. In 2015 Alan published **"Retiring to Our Garden – Year Two"** published this time by Rainbow Publications UK. He then re-issued his first two books this time in a **"Second Edition"**. Also published by Rainbow Publications UK. In 2016 Alan published: **"Skiathos a Greek Island Paradise", "Norfolk the County of my Birth", "Art Inspired by a Rainbow", "Ibiza Island of Dreams", "Majorca Island in the Sun", "Flip-flops and Shades on Thassos", "Mardle and a Troshin' in Norfolk", "England the Country of my Birth", "Mousehole the Cornish Jewel", "Sunshine and Shades on Kefalonia", "Shades and Flip-flops on Zakynthos" and finally "Trips into my Mind's Eye"** Also published by Rainbow Publications UK..

In 2018 and 2019 Alan published the following new books entitled: **"Corfu and Mainland Greece", "Crete and the Island of Santorini", "Cyprus the Pyramids and the Holy Land", "Greek Islands in the Sun", "Being Greek - The Culture of the People of Greece", "Greece Land of Gods and Men". and finally "Alan's Art Books".** Also published by Rainbow Publications UK.

Books by the same Author
Retiring to the Garden – Year 1

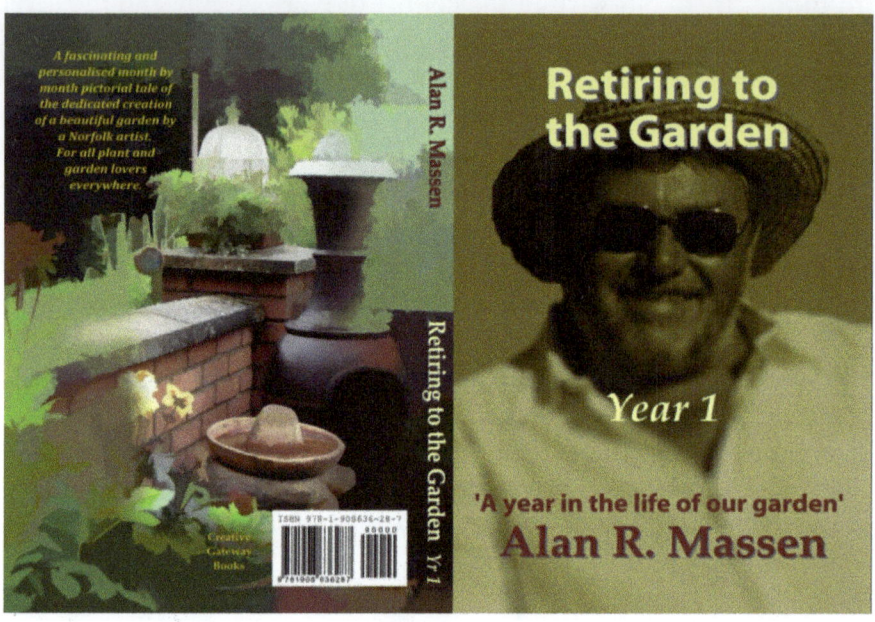

Retiring to Our Garden – Year 1 - 2nd Edition

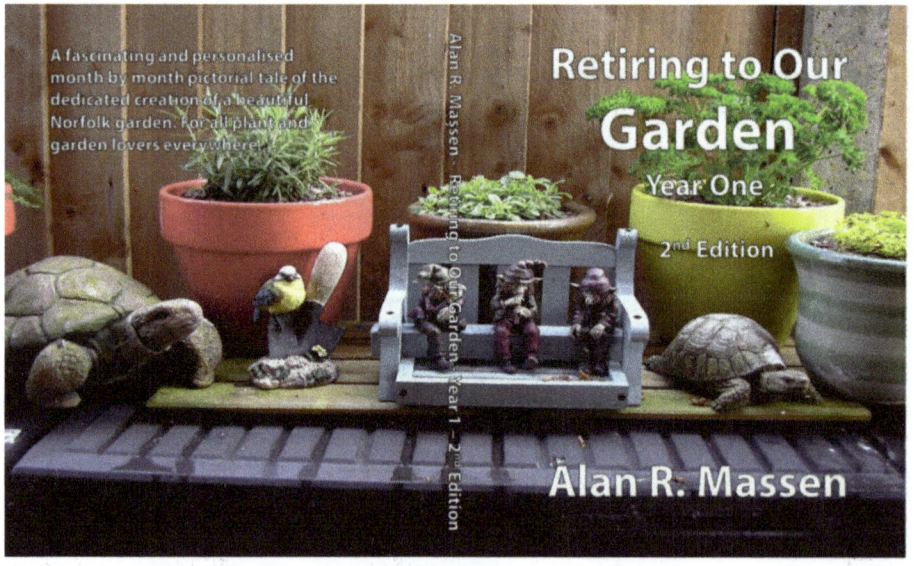

by Norfolk watercolour artist - Alan R. Massen.
Published in Great Britain by Creative Gateway and Rainbow Publications UK

Books by the same Author
Retiring into a Rainbow - 2nd Edition

Retiring to Our Garden – Year Two

by Norfolk watercolour artist - Alan R. Massen.
Published 1st Edition by Creative Gateway and 2nd Edition by Rainbow Publications UK

Books by the same Author

Skiathos a Greek Island Paradise

Norfolk the County of my Birth

by Norfolk watercolour artist - Alan R. Massen.
Published in Great Britain by Rainbow Publications UK

Books by the same Author

Ibiza Island of Dreams

Majorca Island in the Sun

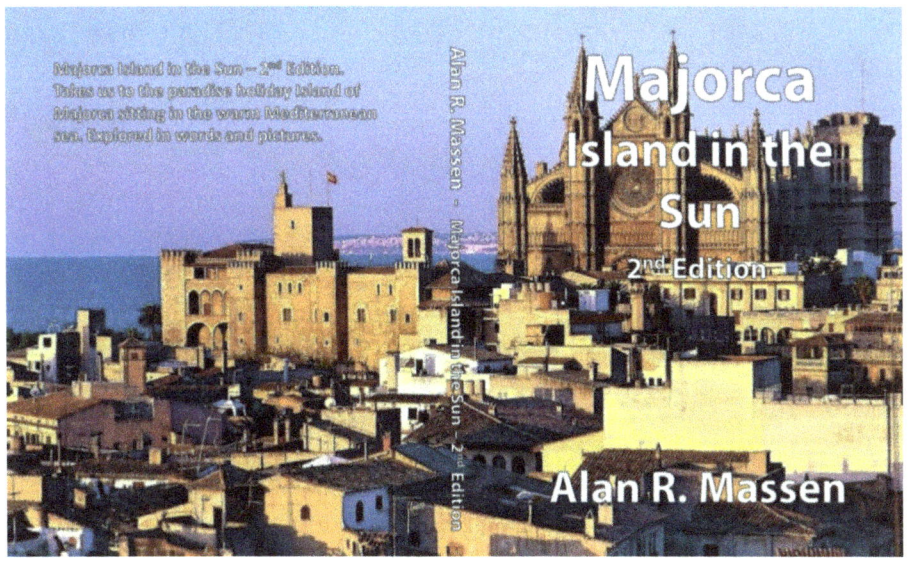

By Norfolk Watercolour Artist - Alan R. Massen
Published in Great Britain by Rainbow Publications UK

Books by the same Author

Art Inspired by a Rainbow

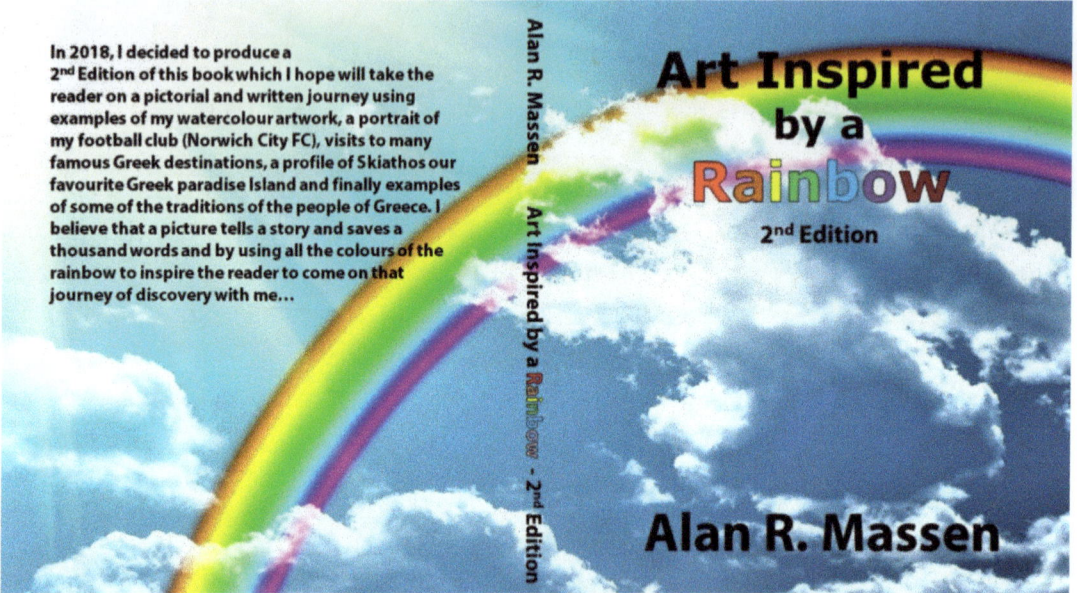

Flip-flops and Shades on Thassos

By Norfolk Watercolour Artist - Alan R. Massen
Published in Great Britain by Rainbow Publications UK

Books by the same Author

Mardle and a Troshin' in Norfolk

Being Greek - The Culture of the People of Greece

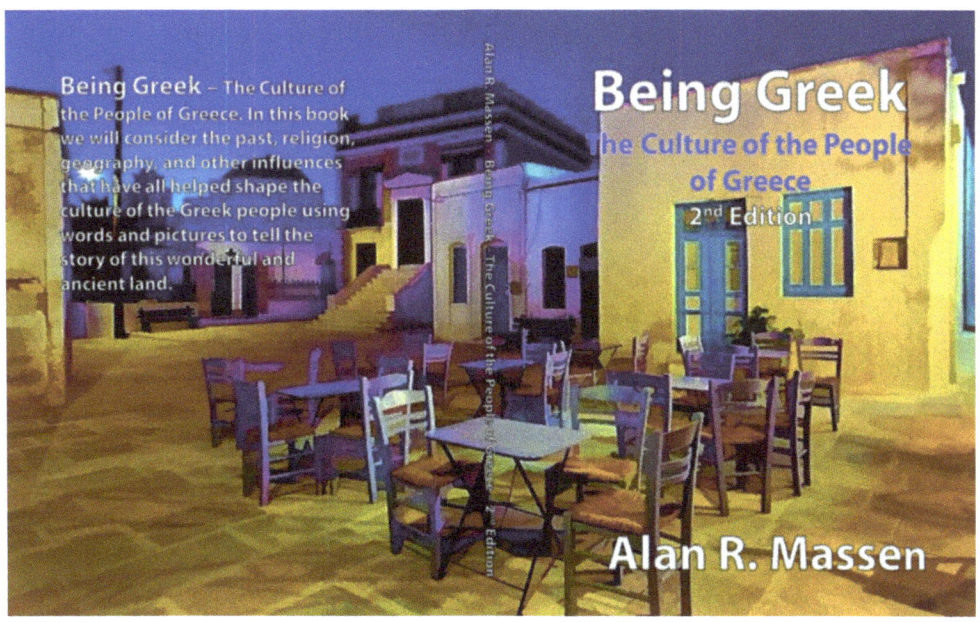

By Norfolk Watercolour Artist - Alan R. Massen
Published in Great Britain by Rainbow Publications UK

Books by the same Author

England the Country of my Birth

Greek Islands in the Sun

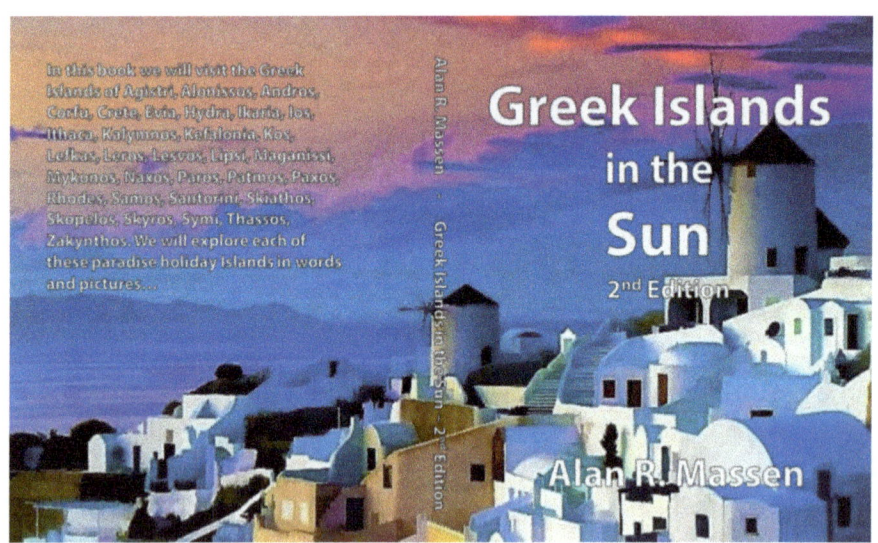

By Norfolk Watercolour Artist - Alan R. Massen
Published in Great Britain by Rainbow Publications UK

Books by the same Author

Mousehole the Cornish Jewel

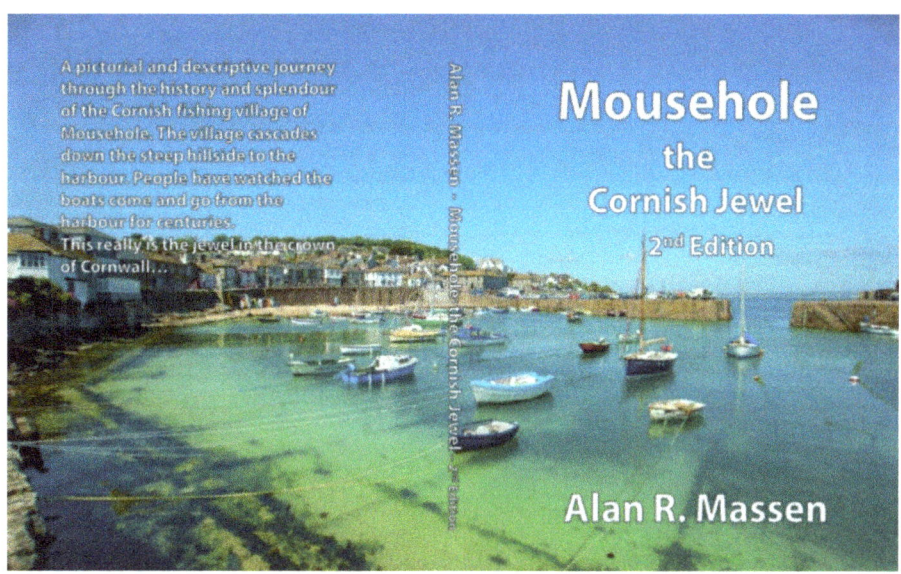

Crete and the Island of Santorini

By Norfolk Watercolour Artist - Alan R. Massen
Published in Great Britain by Rainbow Publications UK

Books by the same Author

Sunshine and Shades on Kefalonia

Shades and Flip-flops on Zakynthos

By Norfolk Watercolour Artist - Alan R. Massen
Published in Great Britain by Rainbow Publications UK

Books by the same Author

Corfu and Mainland Greece

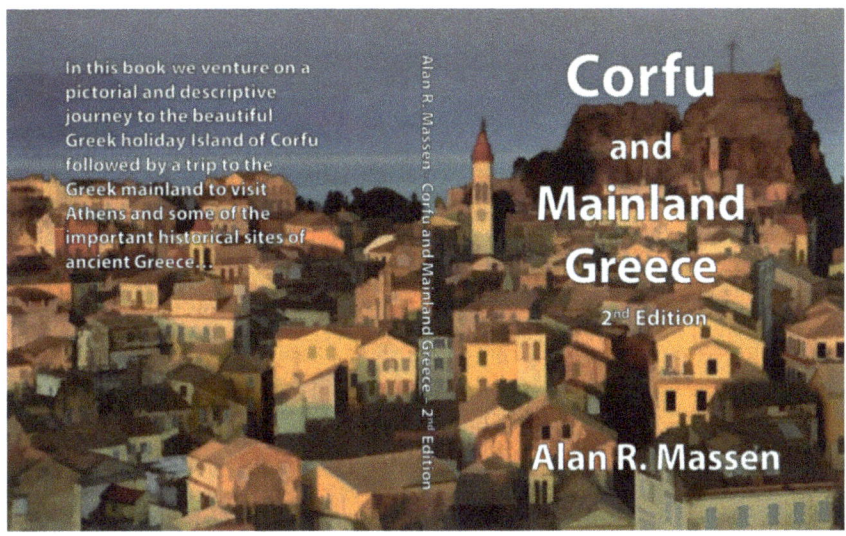

Cyprus the Pyramids and the Holy Land

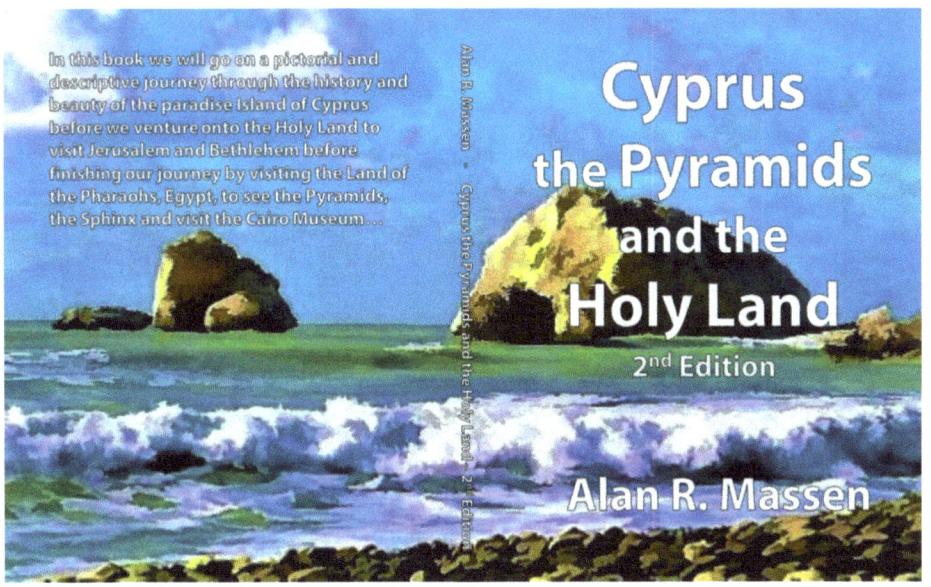

By Norfolk Watercolour Artist - Alan R. Massen
Published in Great Britain by Rainbow Publications UK

Books by the same Author

Trips into my Minds Eye

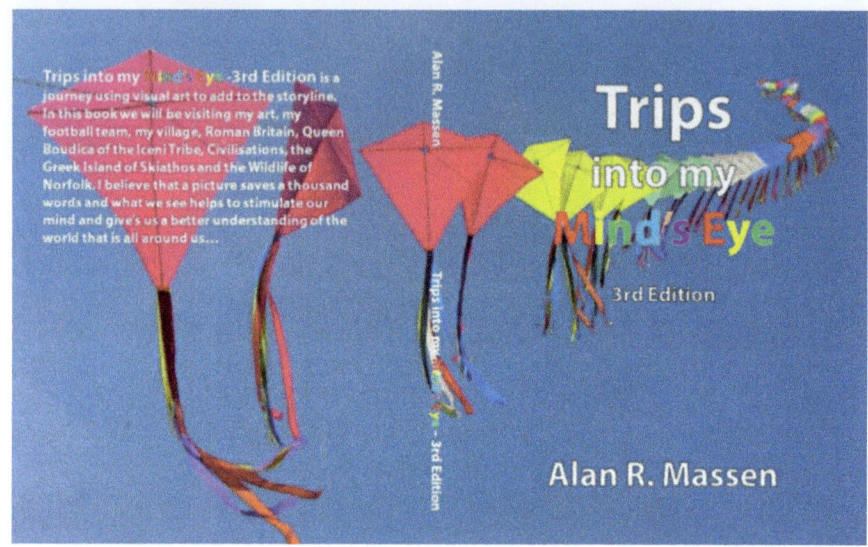

Greece Land of Gods and Men

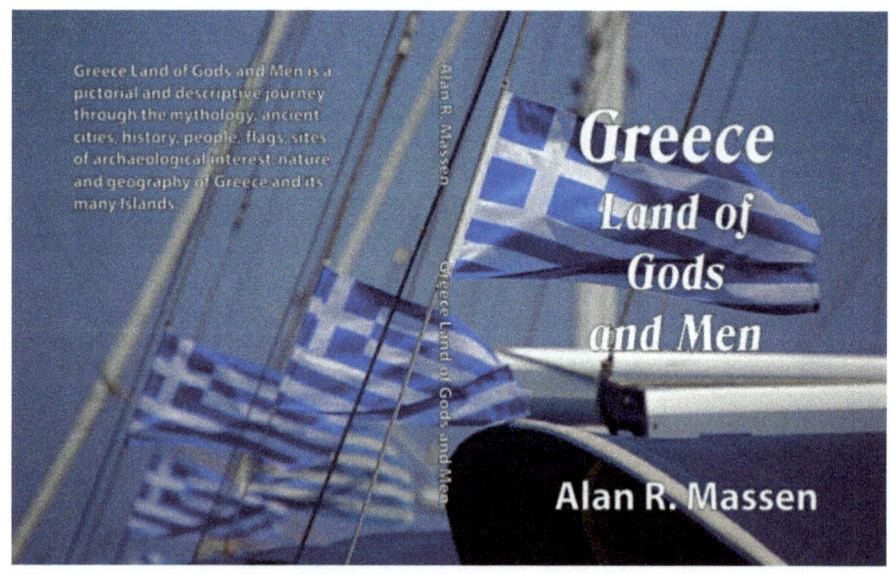

By Norfolk Watercolour Artist - Alan R. Massen
Published in Great Britain by Rainbow Publications UK

Dedication

I would like to dedicate this book to our daughters Mandy, Ginny, our friends Andrew, Lynn, Karl, Anna, Alistair, Issy and my late Mum, Dad and son Paul.

A special mention also to my wife Susie who accompanies me on all our journeys around the UK and abroad and helps me to enjoy, to the full, my life every single day.

Latest book by the same Author

Alan's Art Books

Copyright © 2019 Alan R. Massen

by Norfolk Watercolour Artist - Alan R. Massen
Published in Great Britain by Rainbow Publications UK

Contents

Alan in the Sea on Holiday

Introduction	1
The History of Cyprus	12
The Facts About Cyprus	18
Out and About on Cyprus	44
The City of Nicosia	84
Places to Visit on Cyprus	89
The Best Beaches on Cyprus	109
The Holiday Voyage	123
Cyprus in Colour	153
Acknowledgement	202

Copyright © 2019 Alan R. Massen

Introduction

Cyprus, officially the Republic of Cyprus, is an Island country in the Eastern Mediterranean Sea, off the coasts of Syria and Turkey. Cyprus is the third largest and third most populous Island in the Mediterranean, and has been a member state of the European Union since May 1st 2004. It is located 40 miles south of Turkey, west of Syria and Lebanon, northwest of Israel and Palestine and north of Egypt. This location makes it an ideal holiday destination where the visitor can enjoy the history and beauty of the Island of Cyprus and/or spend some time visiting the Holy Land and the Giza Pyramids of Egypt as part of their holiday experience. This is exactly what we did when we stayed on the Paradise Island of Cyprus at the beautiful resort of Paphos…

Introduction:

Cyprus is a country in its own right and is located in the far eastern edge of Europe in the Mediterranean. There is a wealth of accommodation on Cyprus to suit all travellers including budget lodging, travel lodges, bed and breakfast and luxury hotels. Places to visit on the Island of Cyprus are endless and there is something here to suit everyone with a wealth of historic sites, walking trails, museums, landmarks, monuments, festivals, carnivals and quality shopping. We will be visiting the great beaches, towns and villages on the Paradise Island of Cyprus before going on a journey of discovery to visit the Holy Land Cities of Jerusalem and Bethlehem before then sailing onto see the Giza Pyramids, the Sphinx and visit the fabulous Cairo Museum in Egypt then we return to Cyprus in Colour…

Introduction:

Sailing...

All tied Up…

In this book you will see numerous examples of my watercolour paintings and photographic artwork, like the sailing and all tied up paintings featured above, which I have scanned onto my computer to produce the illustrations that I have used extensively throughout this book. I believe that a picture saves a thousand words and helps transport the reader to faraway places. So if you are comfortable and ready we will begin our journey of discovery together…

Introduction:

Alan…

So now we know where the Island of Cyprus is and just before we venture to far into the pages of this book, I thought, that I ought to introduce myself for those of you that have not been with me on one of my many other journeys to visit other Mediterranean Islands with me. Hello my name is Alan and I am married to Susie, we live in a small Norfolk village in the UK. Together, over the last twenty years, we have been fortunate enough to have had numerous summer holidays abroad. In this time our holiday destination of choice, has usually been to go to one of the many of the Islands in the Mediterranean. We have, over the years, been lucky to have been able to holiday on Cyprus, Majorca, Ibiza, Corfu, Zakynthos, Ithaca, Crete, Santorini, Thassos, Kefalonia and Skiathos to name but a few. We have also had the good fortune to be able to visit the major archaeological sites on the mainland of Greece, Egypt and in the Holy Land. Now that I have introduced myself we will start our journey of discovery by returning once more to the introduction to the beautiful Paradise Island of Cyprus…

Introduction:

Susie and Alan

Cyprus is an island of legends that basks year-round in the light of the warm Mediterranean sun. It has a history that stretches back more than 10,000 years. It has seen civilizations come and go and been visited by the likes of Alexander the Great. Queen Cleopatra of ancient Egypt has ruled here. It is also true that attractive people have always featured prominently in the folklore and history of the Island. It is said that the Greek Goddess Aphrodite made her home on Cyprus, and travellers throughout antiquity (right up to the present day) have come to the Island of Cyprus to pay her tribute and enjoy all the many pleasures that the Island has to offer…

Introduction:

The Island of Cyprus today is a modern country that effortlessly marries European culture with ancient enchantment. Here you will discover a compact world of alluring beaches and fragrant mountain peaks, vineyards studded with olive trees and ancient ruins that stir the imagination, citrus groves and old stone villages where sweet wine flows as freely as conversations at the local café. A carefree place where a sense of timelessness is magnified by the kindness of its people…

Introduction:

The Rock of Aphrodite

The Island is the legendary birthplace of Aphrodite. Cyprus is every inch the Mediterranean hotspot with its sandy beaches, ancient monasteries, classical ruins, thyme scented mountains, terracotta houses and, of course, the obligatory party resorts full of sun-seeking twenty-something's. Cyprus has always been at the crossroads between Europe and Asia. In ancient times, a succession of empires squabbled over its seaports and mountain fortresses, which guaranteed supremacy over the eastern Mediterranean. These empire-builders left behind an incredible legacy of historical relics: ancient Greek and Roman ruins, Crusader castles, mighty Venetians city walls and towering mosques and minarets left behind by Ottoman invaders…

Introduction:

Until the 1970's, Cyprus was a sleepy backwater, but a devastating civil war saw the Island split into Greek Cypriot and Turkish states. In the south, the Greek Republic of Cyprus grew into a modern European state, while the Turkish north half of the Island remained isolated and recognised only by Turkey and was well off the mainstream tourist radar…

Introduction:

After Partition, tourist development went into overdrive in the Greek half of the island, with the emergence of Ayia Napa, Protaras, Limassol, Paphos and a string of other package holiday resorts along the southern coast of the Island. This is one face of the Island of Cyprus with its whitewashed villas, sunbathers, banana-boat rides, boisterous nightclubs and hordes of young and older people enjoying blistering summer sunshine…

Introduction:

Inland, the old Cyprus endures, with beautiful villages full of UNESCO-listed churches, peaceful mountain trails and vineyards that have been producing good quality wines since ancient times. A similar old-world atmosphere pervades in the divided capital, Lefkosia (Nicosia), where quiet lanes lined with Turkish mosques and Byzantine churches come to a sudden halt at the Green Line, the de facto border between the two enclaves…

Introduction:

Kyrenia Harbour

The north of the Island of Cyprus is something else again, more Turkish than Greek, even down to the menus on restaurant tables, but studded with ancient ruins and dramatic Crusader castles. Cyprus gained independence in 1960 with the charismatic Archbishop Makarios III as the first president. In 1974 Makarios was deposed by a Greek military junta. Within days, Turkish troops invaded the Island, the Greeks failed to respond effectively and only after Turkey had taken control of the northern third of the island was a cease-fire arranged by the United Nations. The Island of Cyprus has remained partitioned ever since by a divide that runs through the heart of its capital Nicosia. In mid-2015 the president of Cyprus Nicos Anastasiades and Turkish-Cypriot leader Mustafa Akinci met and resolved to work towards ending its partition. Recently rampant development has taken place along the coast around Famagusta (Gazimagusa) and Kyrenia (Girne), the remote Karpas Peninsula still offers a journey back in time, where ancient ruins spill out onto golden beaches that still see more sea turtles than human visitors. Cyprus is truly a land of plenty and in the next chapter we will be looking at the history of this fascinating Island…

The History of Cyprus

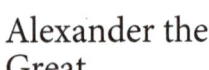
Alexander the Great…

The Island of Cyprus has a long history that incorporates nearly 12,000 years of human activity. It was first inhabited by Neolithic man and subsequently settled by the Mycenaean Greeks from the mainland of Greece, before then being conquered by the Assyrians, Egyptians and Persians then it was seized by Alexander the Great in 333 BC…

The History of Cyprus:

Roman Soldiers

The Island of Cyprus was then incorporated into the Classical Roman Empire then the Eastern Byzantine Empire and following a brief rule by Arab caliphates fell to the English King Richard I. A year later he sold it to the Knights Templar, who in turn re-sold it to the French Lusignans before the Venetians assumed control in the late 15th century. They held it until 1570 when an all-out assault brought it under the control of the Ottoman Empire where it remained for three centuries before being leased to Great Britain in 1878…

The History of Cyprus:

The Ancient Greek God Poseidon

The Island of Cyprus being close to the Suez Canal, the main route to India, under British rule Cyprus became a key military base. After WWI, during which time Cyprus had been formally annexed by Britain, the newly created Turkish republic renounced any claim over Cyprus and in 1925 it became a British colony…

The History of Cyprus:

The Islands Greek and Turkish Cypriots fought on the Allied side during WWII, but after the war nationalists began to agitate for self-determination, either as a nation in its own right, or as part of Greece or Turkey. In the event, Cyprus gained independence in 1960 with the charismatic Archbishop Makarios III as the first president of the new unified Island…

The History of Cyprus:

After 1960 however, the Island remained fraught with ethnic tension and independence fell apart in 1974 when Makarios was deposed by a Greek military junta. Within days, Turkish troops invaded the Island, the Greeks failed to respond effectively and only after Turkey had taken control of the northern third of the island was a cease-fire arranged by the United Nations…

The History of Cyprus:

Aphrodite's Rock and a Greek Cat

The Island of Cyprus has remained partitioned ever since by a divide that runs through the heart of its capital Nicosia. In mid-2015 the president of Cyprus Nicos Anastasiades and Turkish-Cypriot leader Mustafa Akinci met and resolved to work towards ending its partition. Watch this space!

Did you know?

- Legend has it that the Greek goddess of love, Aphrodite, emerged into the World from the surf off what is today known as Aphrodite's Rock beach on Cyprus (see above).

- The Cypriot dessert wine, Commandaria, is the oldest named wine in the World.

- The writer Lawrence Durrell lived on Cyprus from 1952 until 1956.

After reading about the history of Cyprus, in the next chapter, we will, explore some interesting facts about the Island of Cyprus…

Facts About Cyprus

The Religion of Cyprus:

Greek Orthodox is the main religion of the south of Cyprus, with Islam the most prominent religion in the north of the Island.

Social Conventions:

The family, which includes the extended family, is at the centre of Cypriot society. Particular respect is shown to elders. It is not uncommon to see great, great relatives cradling tiny babies, especially at family occasions and festivals. Religious beliefs are also at the core of society and all members of the family are expected to attend church regularly. It is customary to shake hands when greeting, irrespective of whether you have just met or have known the person a long time. Normal courtesies should also be observed. It is viewed as impolite to refuse an offer of Greek coffee or a cold drink. For most occasions, casual attire is acceptable. Beachwear should be confined to the beach or poolside. The Greeks believe that more formal wear is required for business, and in more exclusive dining rooms and at social functions…

Facts about Cyprus:

A Greek Orthodox Priest and a Cypriot harbour

Photography:

Photography is forbidden near military camps or installations. A license from the appropriate authorities is required to photograph museum artefacts. This can sometimes be purchased from the museum's ticket desk. No flash photography is allowed in churches with murals or icons.

Language in Cyprus:

The majority of Cypriots (approximately 80%) speak Greek and approximately 11% speak Turkish. The Greek Cypriot dialect is different from mainland Greek. Turkish is spoken by Turkish Cypriots. English, German and French are also spoken in tourist centres…

Facts about Cyprus:

The Weather on Cyprus:

Cyprus has a sub-tropical climate with sunshine likely on most days of the year. Spring and autumn are pleasantly warm, while summer days are long, dry and hot with temperatures reaching the high 30's and even 40's. The heat is tempered by sea breezes in coastal areas. Winters are mild with often heavy, although sporadic, tropical-style rainstorms. Villages located on higher ground are often subjected to freezing temperatures and frost, while heavy snowfall is experienced in the interior Troodos Mountains and usually stays for several weeks, giving good ski conditions…

Facts about Cyprus:

The Best Time to Visit Cyprus:

The best time to visit for those who like the heat is June, July and August, although the intense sun can make sightseeing a challenge. Drinking lots of bottled water is essential to avoid dehydration. September to January, and April to May, tend to be quieter and are ideal for exploring the island and enjoying pursuits such as cycling and hiking. The ski season on the island generally runs from early February to March…

Facts about Cyprus:

Cloths to Wear on Cyprus:

Pack lightweight, cotton clothing for the summer months, such as loose tops, shorts and linen trousers, along with a hat and sun glasses to protect against the sun. Warmer medium-weight clothing is ideal for spring, autumn and sunny winter days, together with cardigans or jackets for the evenings which can get very cold. Rainwear should be packed for winter visits…

Facts about Cyprus:

The Troodos Mountains on Cyprus

The Geography of Cyprus:

Cyprus is the third-largest island in the Mediterranean and lies to the east at the point where European, Asian and Middle Eastern cultures merge. To the east of the Island is Syria and Lebanon, while to the southeast is Israel and to the west is Greece and its Dodecanese group of Islands. North of Cyprus is Turkey and to the south Egypt…

Facts about Cyprus:

The Geography of Cyprus:

The Island's landscape varies between rugged coastlines with dramatic gorges, bays and sandy beaches, rocky hills, flat plains, river valleys and forest-covered mountains. The Troodos Mountains dominate the interior of the island. Its highest peak is Mount Olympus at 1,952 m (6,400 ft) above sea level. North of Nicosia and following a course towards the barren Karpasia Peninsula runs the mountain range of Pentadaktylos, meaning five fingers after its shape. Between the two is the fertile Mesaoria plain where produce is grown…

Facts about Cyprus:

A village in the Troodos Mountains on Cyprus and Greek Cats

The Geography of Cyprus:

To the west of the Island is the Akamas peninsula, a thickly wooded area that runs from Agios Georgios around the headland to Latsi near Polis. It is home to a vast variety of flora and fauna, many species of which are endemic to Cyprus. In north Cyprus the Morphou basin runs around the coast of Morphou Bay…

Facts about Cyprus:

Flying to Cyprus:

Cyprus is served by international airlines that fly direct to Larnaca International Airport or Paphos International Airport from all around the world. Numerous airlines fly from the UK to Cyprus from many of the airports in the UK...

Facts about Cyprus:

Flying to Cyprus:

All flights to the north of the Island arrive at Ercan International Airport north of Nicosia via Turkey. Turkish Airlines is the Turkish national carrier, with Pegasus Airlines and Atlasglobal among the companies offering flights to north Cyprus…

Facts about Cyprus:

Flying to Cyprus:

While Cyprus is a year-round destination that can boast of attracting tourists who like to relax on the beaches in the morning and ski on snow in the afternoon, at least during the months of February and March, many airlines offer limited flights during the winter. July and August are the most expensive months to fly, while bargains can be found in winter, early spring and late autumn…

Facts about Cyprus:

Flying to Cyprus:

Since 1974, the Cyprus government declared Ercan International Airport an illegal port of entry to Cyprus and there are no direct flights other than from Turkey to the airport. However, tourists can now fly into the south and travel by road across the border in Nicosia to holiday in the north. **Flight Times:** From London Gatwick: to Paphos and Larnaca is 4 hours 30 minutes; to Ercan in north Nicosia, via Turkey is 6 hours (including stopover)…

Facts about Cyprus:

Going by Sea to Cyprus:

The Island of Cyprus has a growing number of marinas that welcome visiting yachts people. Larnaca's marina is the largest. Since 1974, the Cyprus government has declared the ports of Famagusta (Ammochostos) and Kyrenia, both in the north of the Island, as illegal ports of entry into Cyprus…

Facts about Cyprus:

Going by Sea to Cyprus on Cruise Ships:

Cyprus is a regular port of call for cruise companies with eastern Mediterranean itineraries. Cruise ships disembark at the cruise terminal in Limassol. Local companies, Salamis Cruise Lines and Celestyal Cruises offer short cruises of between one and nine days departing from Limassol to Egypt, the Holy Land and Lebanon. These are popular short cruises, with longer cruise options including sailing around the Greek Islands. **Ferry Operators:** Akgünler Denizcilik operates crossings between Taşucu in Turkey and Girne in Northern Cyprus. There are currently no ferries connecting Cyprus with Greece…

Facts about Cyprus:

Where to Stay on Cyprus:

Cyprus has a wide choice of accommodation to suit all budgets and tastes. It boasts some beautiful luxury five-star hotels and holiday resorts with facilities that include pools, playgrounds and even bowling alleys, to hotel apartments, villas, rural guesthouses and agro-tourism stone houses. Most of the top-end hotels - those with a four-star or five-star rating - can be found in Limassol, Larnaca and Paphos and include international restaurants, some of the best thalassotherapy spas in the Mediterranean region, infinity pools, bars and even golf courses. In Nicosia, the upmarket hotels are geared more towards business with conference and meeting facilities provided…

Facts about Cyprus:

Where to Stay on Cyprus:

North Cyprus has a growing number of higher graded hotels with a range of facilities that often include a casino. In the Troodos Mountains, a handful of hotels provide a great base for hiking and cycling enthusiasts, as do the many converted village houses that have been turned into guesthouses or agro-tourism accommodation. Most hotels and hotel apartments in seaside resorts offer discounts during the low season - generally November to March – while mountain resorts can represent excellent value for money with special rates in the winter months. There are often discounts for children occupying the same room as their parents, and some hotels may only charge 80% of the daily room rate for single occupancy of a double room. The Islands hotels in Cyprus are graded deluxe 5-star to 1-star, while hotel apartments and guesthouses are classified A, B or C…

Facts about Cyprus:

Where to Stay on Cyprus:

The trend for bed and breakfast accommodation has largely bypassed Cyprus, with mainly private entrepreneurs offering this option. Most bed and breakfast guesthouses are located in the rural regions of Limassol, Paphos, Larnaca, Akamas and in the Troodos Mountains…

Facts about Cyprus:

Alykes Hala Sultan Teke Mosque Cyprus and a Greek Cat

Where to Stay on Cyprus:

Cyprus has a limited number of camp sites, and those that are available have few facilities. All are licensed by the Cyprus Tourism Organisation. Other accommodation: Guest houses run by families can be found in many rural locations and offer a great way to meet locals. Self-catering villas are often ideal for families on a budget or who wish to have the opportunity to dine out in tavernas. Cyprus has a growing number of agro-tourism premises, which tend to be traditional stone houses that have been restored and converted into tasteful accommodation…

Facts about Cyprus:

The Health Services of Cyprus:

Free emergency treatment is offered to all international tourists at the island's government hospitals' Accident and Emergency Department. Further free or reduced-cost medical treatment is available to European residents who should produce a valid European Health Insurance Card (EHIC) issued by their country of residence's health authority. Note that a European Health Insurance Card (EHIC) is not valid in the Turkish part of Cyprus. It is also advisable to check the working of any private medical insurance policy you purchase to ensure it is valid in Northern Cyprus…

Facts about Cyprus:

The Health Services of Cyprus:

All visitors are advised to purchase additional medical insurance for the duration of their stay, and should have access to funds to cover the cost of treatments. Receipts are issued to reclaim costs back from your insurance company. The island has private medical centres where health and cosmetic treatments are offered. They can be found in all the main towns. Dental services are not free and visitors should have medical insurance that covers emergency treatment…

Facts about Cyprus:

Food and Drink on Cyprus:

Milk on the Island is pasteurised and tap water is generally safe to drink. Bottled water is widely available from supermarkets and kiosks. As with all destinations, it is advisable to eat well-cooked fish and meat, especially chicken and pork which are staples on all hotel and restaurant menus. It is recommended that vegetables should be cooked and fruit produce washed in fresh clean water or peeled before eating…

Facts about Cyprus:

Other Health Risks on Cyprus:

On Cyprus temperatures can be very high and the sun's rays very strong, especially in the summer months. It is advisable to stay out of the sun around midday and wear a hat, sunglasses and a good, high factor sunscreen at all times to protect your skin against sunburn. Remember to always drink plenty of water to avoid dehydration…

Facts about Cyprus:

Currency Information:

The currency in the Republic of Cyprus is the Euro = 100 cents. Notes are in denominations of 500, 200, 100, 50, 20, 10 and 5. Coins are in denominations of 2 and 1, and 50, 20, 10, 5, 2 and 1 cents. The currency used in Northern Cyprus is the Turkish Lira = 100 kuruş. Notes are in denominations of 200, 100, 50, 20, 10 and 5. Coins are in denominations of 1, and 50, 25, 10, 5 and 1 kuruş. Euros, Pounds Sterling and US dollars are generally accepted in the north…

Facts about Cyprus:

Credit Cards:

All major credit cards, such as Visa, Master-Card, Diners Club and American Express, are accepted at larger restaurants and shops, and in hotels. Smaller shops, such as those in villages, and rural tavernas are unlikely to accept credit cards. Entry to museums and tourist attractions are payable in cash. As of early 2013 credit and debit cards may be less accepted on the Island, due to ongoing capital controls imposed on the banks…

Facts about Cyprus:

ATM's:

There are reliable ATM's in the main Towns and tourist areas on the Island of Cyprus. As of early 2013, withdrawals from Cypriot banks are limited due to the ongoing capital controls imposed on the banks throughout the country. Carrying cash, rather than relying on cards, is therefore, a very good idea…

Facts about Cyprus:

Travellers Cheque's:

On the Island of Cyprus cheque's may be cashed in all banks. To avoid additional exchange rate charges, travellers are advised to take traveller's cheque's in Euros. **Banking Hours:** South Cyprus: Mon-Fri 0815-1330. North Cyprus: Mon-Fri 0800-1200 and 1400-1600. All banks on the Island are closed on public holidays. Now that we have read about some of the facts about the Island we will, in the next chapter, go out and about on Cyprus and explore…

Out and About on Cyprus

The Akamas Peninsula

With its rugged un-spoilt landscape of woods of pine trees and sandy bays, the Akamas Peninsula (see above) is a wonderful place to escape the crowds and be with nature. It stretches from the harbour at Agios Georgios, north of Paphos, to Chrysochou Bay near Polis, and is famous for its diverse and wonderful wildlife and its rare, endemic flora…

Out and About on Cyprus:

Nicosia

The Cyprus Museum

A visit to the Cyprus Museum with its magnificent collection of archaeological treasures dating back to Neolithic times is a must for all Island visitors. Collections include astonishingly well-preserved Mycenaean pottery, Chalcolithic figurines, Egyptian and Roman statues, and carvings from the Royal Tombs at Salamis. The museum is located in central Nicosia…

Out and About on Cyprus:

The Theatre at Kourion Limassol

At Kourion there is a spectacular Greco-Roman theatre, agora (marketplace) and the remains of a cathedral, plus a villa, the House of Eustolios, with its well-preserved 5th century floor mosaics, the ancient City-Kingdom site of the Kourion is the finest archaeological site on the Island. On the same site there is also a stadium and a sanctuary…

Out and About on Cyprus:

Kyrenia Town

The Town of Kyrenia was once an important Roman and Venetian port and was said to be one of the most picturesque harbours in the Mediterranean. Kyrenia is a very busy north Cyprus Town dominated by a vast fortress. The castle at Kyrenia houses a Shipwreck Museum, which is best known for its 2,300-year-old merchant vessel and amphorae…

Out and About on Cyprus:

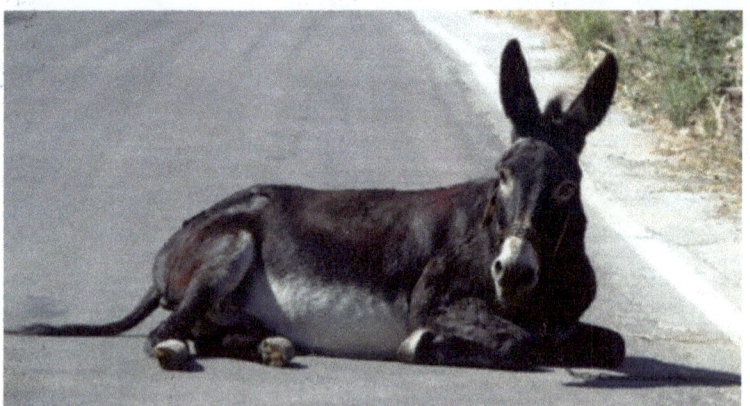

Lefkara Village

This charming village between Limassol and Larnaca on Cyprus is famous for its silver filigree and, significantly, its lace. Legend has it that the Italian painter Leonardo da Vinci visited Lefkara in the 15th century and purchased some of its lefkaritika lace for the cathedral in Milan, and in doing so secured its fame…

Out and About on Cyprus:

The Petra tou Romiou (The Rock of Aphrodite)

A landmark of Cyprus and said to be where the Greek goddess Aphrodite was born, Petra tou Romiou (Rock of Aphrodite) is one of the most beautiful spots on the Island. Turquoise seawater surrounds the rock. Nearby, is the Temple of Aphrodite on the site of the ancient City of Palaipafos…

Out and About on Cyprus:

The Phoinikoudes Esplanade in Larnaca

The 3 km (2 miles) or so long esplanade that is lined with palm trees, the Phoinikoudes (locally Foinikoudes) is the icon image of Larnaca. Here, visitors can relax on the beach or dine on seafood while looking out over the Mediterranean Sea. At one end of the esplanade lies Larnaca's marina and at the other its famous fort…

Out and About on Cyprus:

The Tombs of the Kings in Paphos

Dating from the ancient Hellenistic and Roman period, this collection of rock cut tombs have helped to earn Paphos UNESCO World Heritage status. The tombs were of noblemen, rather than Kings, and are historically important because of their design; some resemble houses with a Peristyle atrium courtyard…

Out and About on Cyprus:

The Painted Churches of Troodos

In the Troodos area dating back to Byzantine times, this collection of 10 richly painted churches and tiny monasteries are a UNESCO World Heritage Site. Two of the most spectacular are the Agios Nikolaos tis Stegis at Kakopetria with frescos from the 11th century, and Panagia tou Araka with scenes from the Old Testament…

Out and About on Cyprus:

The Resort of Ayia Napa

Once the hedonistic capital of the Island of Cyprus, Ayia Napa has 'grown up' and now has a growing number of sophisticated nightspots, restaurants and cultural venues, as well as lively clubs that attract the young, trendy set. The resort has some of the best beaches and diving opportunities on the Island…

Out and About on Cyprus:

Aphrodite…

The Baths of Aphrodite

An isolated freshwater pool on the edge of the Akamas Peninsula called the Baths of Aphrodite near Polis is where, so legend has it, the Greek goddess bathed and enjoyed having fun with the Greek God Adonis. Today, the natural beauty of the untouched countryside is as much an attraction as the grotto…

Out and About on Cyprus:

The Platres Chocolate Factory

On the Island visitors can indulge their taste buds on the slopes of the Troodos Mountains at the Platres chocolate workshop (see above). The owners import the raw chocolate they use from Venezuela…

Out and About on Cyprus:

The Hala Sultan Tekke Mosque

Located near Larnaca International Airport on the Island, the Hala Sultan Tekke is a beautiful 19th century mosque set amongst palm trees. It overlooks Larnaca's Salt Lake where migratory flamingos stay in the winter. Considered to be one of the most sacred Muslim shrines, the mosque contains an ancient tomb and is a place of pilgrimage…

Out and About on Cyprus:

The Kourion Ancient Site in Limassol

I have already mentioned this site in this book but it is well worth featuring again because the Kourion with its spectacular Greco-Roman theatre, agora (marketplace) and the remains of a cathedral, plus a villa, the House of Eustolios, with well-preserved 5th century floor mosaics, the ancient City-Kingdom site of the Kourion is the finest archaeological site on Cyprus. On the same site there is also a stadium and a sanctuary. It is a must visit site for all those who love history…

Out and About on Cyprus:

The Kykkos Monastery

The Kykkos Monastery is the largest and most famous monastery on the Island of Cyprus. Founded in 1100 by the Byzantine emperor Alexios Komnenos, the monastery is dedicated to the Virgin Mary and is home to one of the three surviving icons painted by the Apostle Luke. Kykkos Monastery is ornately decorated and covered in a silver gilt, enclosed in a tortoiseshell shrine. It is also famous for its museum, located within the monastery grounds, which houses an impressive collection of icons, woodcarvings and manuscripts, and other Cypriot antiquities. The nearby Troodos Mountains, with its magnificent hills and valleys, should also be explored as they are home to nine Byzantine churches, included on the UNESCO World Heritage list, and richly decorated with murals and Byzantine paintings…

Out and About on Cyprus:

The Harbour at Paphos

In the Town of Paphos is the beautiful medieval fort (see above) that dominates the picturesque harbour. It is well worth seeing anytime of the year, but particularly during the summer festival when operatic sounds reverberate around its ancient walls. Nearby, you can see the Paphos world-famous mosaics that show scenes from Greek mythology. We have had a great holiday in this beautiful resort and we loved it…

Out and About on Cyprus:

The Old Town of Paphos

When we holidayed on Cyprus our hotel was in the Old Town of Paphos and we enjoyed wandering around the Old Town, harbour and visiting the ancient sites nearby. The food served in the local tavernas was delicious and very traditional. Paphos was a great base for our stay on the island…

Out and About on Cyprus:

The Goddess Aphrodite at Paphos

The Greeks have agreed that Aphrodite had landed at the site of Paphos when she arose from the sea. Her worship was introduced to Paphos from Syria or much more probably it was of Phoenician origin. Before it was proved by archaeology it was understood that the cult of Aphrodite had been established before the time of Homer (c. 700 BC), as the grove and altar of Aphrodite at Paphos are mentioned in the Odyssey. Archaeology has established that Cypriots venerated a fertility goddess before the arrival of the Greeks on the Island, in a cult that combined Aegean and eastern mainland aspects. Female figurines and charms found in the immediate vicinity date as far back as the early third millennium. The sanctuary to her fell into non-use and all that is left is the ruins we see today…

Out and About on Cyprus:

The Medusa

In Greek mythology Medusa was a monster, a Gorgon, generally described as a winged human female with a hideous face and living venomous snakes in place of hair. Gazers upon her face would turn to stone.

The Goddess Aphrodite at Paphos

At the Paphos sanctuary the worship of the goddess was focused, not for Cyprus alone, but for the whole Aegean world. The Cinyradae, or descendants of Cinyras, were the chief priests, Greek by name but of Phoenician origin. Their power and authority was very great; but it may be inferred from certain inscriptions that they were controlled by a senate and an assembly of the people. There was also an oracle based here. Few places have ever been so much sung and glorified about by the poets than Paphos. The remains of the vast temple of Aphrodite are still discernible, its circumference marked by huge foundation walls. After its destruction by an earthquake it was rebuilt by Vespasian, on whose coins it is shown, as well as on earlier and later coins…

Out and About on Cyprus:

The Disciple Paul in Paphos

According to the biblical Acts of the Apostles, after landing at Salamis and proclaiming the Word of God in the synagogues, the prophets and teachers, Barnabas and Saul of Tarsus, travelled along the entire southern coast of the Island of Cyprus until they reached Paphos. There, Serius Paulus, the Roman proconsul, was converted. In Paphos, Acts first identifies Saul as the disciple Paul…

Out and About on Cyprus:

The New Town of Paphos

New Paphos (Nea Paphos), the currently inhabited town, was founded by the sea, near the western end of the Island, and possessed a good harbour. It lay's about 60 stadia or 12 km northwest of the old city. It, too, had a founding myth: it was said to have been founded by Agapenor, chief of the Arcadians at the siege of Troy, who, after the capture of that town, was driven by the storm that separated the Greek fleet, onto the coast of the Island of Cyprus. At this time, Pausanias VIII, an Agapenor was mentioned as King of the Paphians. Like its ancient namesake, Nea Paphos was also distinguished for the worship of Aphrodite and contained several magnificent temples dedicated to her. The old city sanctuary seems to have always retained its preeminence in this respect with the road leading to it from Nea Paphos being annually crowded with worshipers making their way to the more ancient shrine…

Out and About on Cyprus:

The New Town of Paphos

Paphos is mentioned as having been visited by Paul of Tarsus, when it appears to have been the residence of the Roman governor; it is said that Paul converted the governor to Christianity. A visit of the youthful Titus to Paphos before he acceded to the Roman Empire, who inquired with much curiosity into its history and antiquities. Under this name the historian doubtless included the ancient as well as the more modern city: and among other traits of the worship of the temple he records, with something like surprise, that the only image of the goddess was a pyramidal stone. There are still considerable ruins of New Paphos remaining a mile or two from the sea; among which are the remains of three temples…

Out and About on Cyprus:

The Saint Hilarion Castle near Kyrenia

The magnificent ruins of Saint Hilarion castle tower out of the limestone rocks of the mountains overlooking Kyrenia. Its turrets and walls built on sheer rock make it one of the finest sights in northern Cyprus. The castle still has the remains of its chapel, royal apartments, banqueting hall, courtyards and stables. There is skiing in the surrounding mountains which usually lasts from January to mid-March, but the Troodos Mountains resort is actually the nearest to the skiing area. In the Troodos Mountains there are spectacular scenery where you can enjoy hiking and cycling trails, nature reserves, churches and the famous Kykkos Monastery. In winter, resorts offer skiing on the snow-covered peaks, including Mount Olympus, which at 1,952 m (6,404 ft) above sea level, is the Island's highest point…

Out and About on Cyprus:

The Saint Hilarion Castle near Kyrenia

The Saint Hilarion Castle lies on the Kyrenia mountain range, on the Island of Cyprus. This location provided the castle with command of the road that led through the pass from Kyrenia to Nicosia. It is the best preserved ruin of the three former strongholds in the Kyrenia mountains, the others being Kantara and Buffavento. Saint Hilarion was originally a monastery, named after a monk who allegedly chose the site for his hermitage, with a monastery and a church built there in the 10th century. Starting in the 11th century, the Byzantines began fortification. Saint Hilarion formed the defences of the Island with the castles of Buffavento and Kantara against the Arab pirates that were raiding the coast of the Island. Some sections of the castle were further upgraded under the Lusignan rule, who may have used it as a summer residence. During the rule of the Lusignans, the castle was the focus of a four-year struggle between the Holy Roman Emperor Frederick II and Regent John d' Ibelin for control of the Island of Cyprus…

Out and About on Cyprus:

The Saint Hilarion Castle near Kyrenia

The castle has three divisions or wards. The lower and middle wards served economic purposes, while the upper ward housed the royal family. The lower ward had the stables and the living quarters for the men-at arms. The Prince John tower sits on a cliff high above the lower castle. The church lies on the middle ward. The upper ward was reserved for the Royals and can be entered via a well-preserved archway. Farm buildings are located in the west close to the royal apartments. Along the western wall, there is a scenic view of the northern coast of the Island of Cyprus, overlooking the city of Kyrenia, from the Queen's Window. Much of the castle was dismantled by the Venetians in the 15th century to reduce the up-keeping cost of the castle garrison…

Out and About on Cyprus:

Shopping on the Island of Cyprus

Many people who visit the Island often make the following Cypriot purchases that include handmade lace, woven curtains and tablecloths, silks, basketwork, pottery, silverware and leather goods. Lefkara lace, known as lefkaritika, is famous throughout the world as one of the products most closely associated with Cypriot workmanship. It is intricately patterned and used for mainly tablecloths and table mats. Women can be seen working in small workshops in the village of Lefkara after which the lace is named. The village is located on a hill just off the Nicosia-Limassol highway. The Troodos village of Omodos also has a thriving lace-making industry. Lefkara is also famous for its silver-work; traditionally the men of the village would work with silver while the women produced lace. The giving of silver spoons and forks are a traditional symbol of Cypriot hospitality…

Out and About on Cyprus:

Shopping on the Island of Cyprus

On Cyprus the making of jewellery is an art which has been practiced since the Mycenaean Greek period; craftspeople working in contemporary and traditional styles produce some very fine pieces. Filigree silver is a popular gift or souvenir. Local wines, including Commandaria, which is one of the oldest wines in the world and produced in the region north of Limassol, and Cyprus's own brandy and its potent Zivania liqueur also make good purchases. Imported goods sell at competitive prices on the Island, including cameras, perfume, porcelain and crystal. In northern Cyprus, embroidered tablecloths and cushions with patterns traditional to Turkey are widely available…

Out and About on Cyprus:

Shopping on the Island of Cyprus

Throughout the Island of Cyprus, monasteries sell icons, which are often painted by the monks themselves. The Monastery of Chrysorrogiatissa in the foothills of the Troodos Mountains is one of several that has its own icon studio. **Shopping Hours on the Island of Cyprus:** In summer (June to August) shops are open 0800-1400 and 1700-2030. In winter opening hours are 0800-1300 and 1430-1800 (until 1900 in spring and autumn). However many larger department stores and supermarkets, and shops in tourist areas, do not close for lunch. Shops are closed Wednesday and Saturday after 1300, as well as all day on Sunday...

Out and About on Cyprus:

Nightlife on the Island of Cyprus

There is a thriving nighttime scene in the capital Nicosia and the coastal towns and cities of Cyprus. Hundreds of restaurants serving everything from Indian cuisine to Italian, French and Chinese, along with wine bars, lively bars with live entertainment, theatres offering classical plays, cinemas and nightclubs are popular with locals as well as visitors. Restaurants and bars line the seafront of places like Larnaca, Paphos and Limassol, and Kyrenia in northern Cyprus. The party capital of Cyprus remains Ayia Napa where youngsters dance until late, even though the resort is seeing a growing number of restaurants and sophisticated nightspots emerging. Other resorts on the Island have their own good restaurants, bars, tavernas and nightspots…

Out and About on Cyprus:

Nightlife on the Island of Cyprus

Most cities on the Island host regular evening cultural events and festivals. Among the most popular are the Aphrodite operatic festival held in front of the castle in Paphos Harbour and Shakespeare performances at the Kourion. Casinos are a rarity on Cyprus. Gambling venues are steadily opening up throughout the Island, true casinos that offer roulette and poker can be found only in northern Cyprus. Nightlife in the rural villages tends to revolve around the local taverna, but nonetheless can be a lively affair with traditional music and dance…

Out and About on Cyprus:

Food and Drink on the Island of Cyprus

Cypriot cuisine is delicious and healthy, and takes its inspiration from Greece and Turkey. In the south, the cuisine is pure Mediterranean, with fruit, such as olives that can be picked from the trees that fill the Island's landscape and lemons, combined with aromatic herbs from the Troodos Mountains foothills to give intense flavours to chicken, pork, lamb and fish dishes…

Out and About on Cyprus:

Food and Drink on the Island of Cyprus

In Northern Cyprus, the cuisine has all the hallmarks of Middle Eastern and Central Asian cooking, with the extensive use of herbs and spices like saffron and paprika that give strong colours and flavours to meat. Many dishes found in Northern Cyprus are served with sauces made from tomato, yoghurt, and are often served with rice…

Out and About on Cyprus:

Food and Drink on the Island of Cyprus

On the Island of Cyprus all the major holiday resorts have bars, tavernas and restaurants, although the cuisine tends to be international rather than local dishes. The best way to enjoy authentic Cypriot food is to dine in a taverna and order a *mezedhes* (also known as a meze or mezze). You will be rewarded by a steady stream of 20 or more small plates topped with local dishes being brought to your table. Typically, a *mezedhes* will start with dips, such as tzatziki made with yoghurt, cucumber and garlic, or hummus (pureed chickpeas with lemon), accompanied by bread and salad, followed by various meat, fish and vegetable dishes and culminate in fruit or cake…

Out and About on Cyprus:

Food and Drink Specialties of Cyprus

Afelia (pork slow-cooked in red wine and coriander) and **Kleftiko** (slow-cooked lamb with herbs) are two of the most popular regional dishes of the south of the Island, with **Imam Bayildi** (aborigines stuffed with tomato and onions) and **Adana** (skewered minced lamb and red pepper) found on many menus in the north of Cyprus. Other favourite dishes are: **Dolmades** (vine leaves stuffed with meat and/or rice). **Kebabs** (pieces of meat - typically lamb - skewered and roasted over charcoal). **Tava** (a tasty baked stew of lamb, herbs, onions and potatoes). **Stifado** (a casserole of beef or hare cooked with wine, vinegar, onion and spices). Fresh seafood such as **Tsipoura** (seabream), **Lavraki** (seabass) and **Garides** (prawns)…

Out and About on Cyprus:

Eating out on the Island of Cyprus

Evening dinner is the most important meal of the day on the Island and rarely starts before 8 pm. A service charge is added to all bills, and tipping is discretionary. Strong black coffee and wine, which is produced in abundance, are popular drinks in both the south and north of the Island of Cyprus. **Cyprus produces excellent wines, spirits and beers: Zivania** (a strong spirit made from grapes). **Brandy Sour** (cocktail made from Cyprus brandy, soda, lemon squash and angostura bitters) and **Commandaria** (a sweet desert wine dating back to ancient times)…

Out and About on Cyprus:

Getting Around the Island of Cyprus by Road

Exploring the Island by car is the best way to get around. Cyprus's road infrastructure is excellent. The result is a traffic jam-free motorway drive that takes you from Paphos in the east straight into Limassol and on to the centre of Nicosia, plus a branch heading off to Larnaca, Agia Napa and Protaras. Driving in the Troodos Mountains is good, albeit with roads that zig-zag around ravines. Off-road driving should only be done with a suitable vehicle. Drivers wishing to reach the north of Cyprus need to cross the border, known as the Green Line, at one of five designated checkpoints (there are a further two checkpoints in Nicosia for pedestrians only). The Green Line is controlled by UN forces. The five crossings are Limnitis at Kato Pygros, Astromeritis near Morphou, Agios Dometios in Nicosia, Pergamos at Pyla and Strovilia near Agios Nikolaos. In Nicosia you can cross on foot at the Ledra Palace checkpoint and Ledra Street in the centre of the city…

Out and About on Cyprus:

Getting Around the Island of Cyprus by Road

Remember that on the Island of Cyprus they drive on the left hand side of the road just like us back in the UK. **Road Quality:** Motorways and main roads are of a high standard. Inner city and smaller town roads are generally good, but infrastructure upgrades have resulted in uneven surfaces. Roads in villages are often poor. All roads on the Island are toll free…

Out and About on Cyprus:

A Hawk flying over Cyprus

Getting Around the Island of Cyprus by Road

Cyprus has car hire companies with offices in the airports and towns, including major names like Hertz and Europcar. Cars should be reserved well in advance during the summer season. You should be sure to check your agreement if you are planning to take a hired car across the Green Line as not all hire companies in the south permit visitors to take their vehicles to northern Cyprus. The minimum driving age is 18, but drivers often need to be 21 years old and to have held a valid licence for three years to hire a car on the Island…

Out and About on Cyprus:

Getting Around the Island of Cyprus by road from Paphos Airport

The second largest airport on the Island of Cyprus, Paphos International Airport provides easy road access to the western part of the Island. The Paphos International Airport guide includes information on terminal facilities, contact details, transportation options and nearby hotels. There is a tourist information desk in the terminal building. If you are driving from the resort of Paphos, take the B6 to the southeast and turn onto the E603 after about 12 km (7.5 miles). From here, Paphos International Airport is clearly signposted. Taxis are available from the taxi rank outside of the terminal building. …

Out and About on Cyprus:

Bus Transport in the Resort of Paphos

The local bus company run regular services from early morning until late evening on weekdays between the Harbour Station in central Paphos and the bus station opposite the airport terminal (journey time: 30 minutes). Services start later and finish earlier from December to March. Bus connections to various destinations in the region and other parts of the Island of Cyprus are available from the main bus terminal in Paphos…

The City of Nicosia

Nicosia is the capital of the Island of Cyprus, a status it has enjoyed for a 1,000 years since the 10th century, though its beginnings date back 5,000 years to the Bronze Age. It lies roughly in the centre of the Island in the Mesaoria Plain, flanked by the beautiful northern range of the Kyrenia Mountains. It is called locally the Pentadaktylos or the five finger mountain. There are various suggestions as to the origin of the name Nicosia - or 'Lefkosia' In Greek - but the most likely one is linked to the popular tree, the tall Lefka trees that once adorned the city...

The City of Nicosia:

You should always
Find the time
for a Coffee
Break on
Cyprus…

Nicosia is the seat of government, diplomatic headquarters and cultural centre of the Island of Cyprus, the capital presents two distinct faces: the old, original part of the city, surrounded by sturdy Venetian walls over 400 years old, and a busy modern metropolis which has a population of more than 171,000 people when you include its suburbs. Within the large area encircled by the strong bastion walls that served to protect the town for centuries are many places of great historic interest. The central Eleftheria Square links old Nicosia with the elegant modern city that has grown up outside the walls, where hotels, offices, restaurants and gardens blend happily with the fine old houses and colonial buildings of this beautiful cosmopolitan city…

The City of Nicosia:

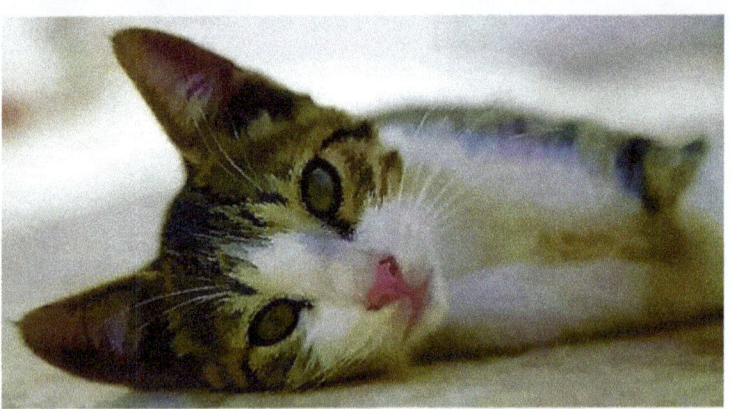

Nicosia is without a doubt the largest city on the Island of Cyprus, located at the centre of the Island. Nicosia serves as home for the oldest and most beautiful museums as well as a theatre for the performing arts. The old part of the city is bordered with parks and remains from the ancient world, while the new city holds its head high with many skyscrapers. Some of the major museums and tourist attractions that Nicosia has to offer are as follows: Cyprus Museum, National Struggle Museum, Nicosia Municipal Arts Centre, Leventis Municipal Museum, Byzantine Museum, Museum of the History of Cypriot Coinage, Ledra Observatory Museum, The Cyprus Classic Motorcycle Museum, The Nicosia Municipal Theatre…

The City of Nicosia:

The national sport of the Island is football and tourists often make their way to the stadiums to watch a game. The National Cyprus Football team has its home ground at the Nicosia stadium. The City of Nicosia is the ideal place to get a taste of the traditional Cypriot cuisine. Nicosia serves mouth-watering food in traditional settings as well as the newly developed love for McDonalds and a majority of the other famous franchises, tourists will find all that they require in Nicosia. For men and women alike, various spas are available for a relaxing massage and if you are looking for a night out at the movies, Nicosia offers an extensive diversity of cinemas as well. All in all, the City is a major tourist spot, bustling with visitors from all over the world, especially during the summertime…

The City of Nicosia:

The walled city of Nicosia is a mix of old and new. Visit the Old Town full of quaint tavernas housed in Venetian mansions. Top attractions include the Archbishop's Palace, the spectacular Byzantine Art Museum, St John's Cathedral with its beautiful frescos, the House of Hadjigeorgiakis Kornesios and the Ömeriye Mosque. Now that we have sampled the delights of the City it is time for us to head for the best places to visit on the Island and that is exactly where we are going in the next chapter…

Places to Visit on Cyprus

The Resort of Ayia Napa

Ayia Napa is one of Europe's most famous party resorts, Ayia Napa, is one of the stars of the Mediterranean Island Nation of Cyprus. With its year-round warm weather and sandy beach it is easy to see why the resort is so popular. In summer the bars and clubs boom with international DJs and holiday-makers from all over Europe, while families are also welcome in this fully fledged resort that has grown rapidly from the simple fishing village it was only a few decades ago. The rest of this holiday Island is also blessed with beaches, resorts and tourist attractions that are easily accessible from Ayia Napa…

Places to Visit on Cyprus:

The Resort of Ayia Napa

Ayia Napa's Nissi Beach is one of the most attractive on the Island of Cyprus, boasting a sweep of very clean golden sand, as well as sun loungers and sun umbrellas for hire. Bars, tavernas, music, banana boat rides and a host of other watersports make this lively stretch of sand popular with the clubbing crowd and has been compared to Bondi Beach. For quieter stretches of beach head out to Cape Greco, to the east of Ayia Napa…

Places to Visit on Cyprus:

The Resort of Ayia Napa

Head away from the resort's beach and enjoy the calm and peace of the Monastery of Ayia Napa. It is best to visit here in the morning before most holidaymaker's have woken up so you can admire the 600-year-old fig tree and marble fountain without the crowds. The monastery dates from as far back as the Venetian days of the 16th century. There are also regular boat trips out from the resort to Cape Greco and the resort of Protaras…

Places to Visit on Cyprus:

The Resort of Ayia Napa

Ayia Napa is a popular resort with families and its beach is the main attraction. Other attractions nearby, include Water World, a fun water park on the resort's outskirts, and the Marine Life Museum, which has a modest collection of shells and preserved sea life including sharks. The resort also features children's play pools, family friendly restaurants and sports facilities like tennis courts are also on hand to ease you through your stay at the resort…

Places to Visit on Cyprus:

Resorts close to Ayia Napa

The popular resort of Protaras is located just east of Ayia Napa. There are buses and boat tours to Protaras with the main attraction the sprinkling of lovely beaches that are dotted in and around the resort. Choose from Agia Triada, Louma, Mouzoura, Pernera and Protaras beach itself. To really get away from it all head to Green Bay Beach, where holidaymaker's go to escape the maddening crowds…

Places to Visit on Cyprus:

The City of Limassol

Bold and energetic Limassol is one of Cyprus's liveliest cities, it has long attracted holidaymaker's to its resort hotels, where sweeping sea views, swimming pools and private stretches of beach are all available. Limassol also boasts a compact and charming old Town, a palm-fringed promenade backed by long and thin sandy beaches and cooling seawater. The warren of streets that flank the seaside front have an allure all of their own and are crammed with cafés, tavernas, trendy bars, lively nightclubs and shops selling everything from souvenirs to the latest fashions. This is a real city where tourists and locals mingle happily. After a hard day's shopping, relaxing on the beach, or tanning by the pool, you will be congratulating yourself over a cool cocktail on taking your holiday in this cosmopolitan resort city…

Places to Visit on Cyprus:

The City of Limassol

The Limassol waterfront is dotted with hotels and public beaches, where you can soak up the sun, or take a cooling dip in the Mediterranean Sea. For the best beaches head away from Limassol to perhaps Ladies Beach, Curium Beach or Pissouri Beach. On these beaches a raft of watersports are on offer ranging from pedaloes to jet-skis…

Places to Visit on Cyprus:

The City of Limassol

Take a stroll along the seaside promenade to Limassol's old Town where the assorted delights of the centuries-old architecture, the city's medieval fort, an archaeological museum, the folk museum and a natural sea sponge exhibition await. This is a great place to enjoy a leisurely lunch, with the old carob warehouse and the other eateries that flank the fort are all good options…

Places to Visit on Cyprus:

The City of Limassol

In Limassol and its environs have plenty to keep the children occupied. Away from the beaches the Wet 'n' Wild and Fasouri waterpark tempt with their slides and pools. In Limassol's old harbour, the residents of the Reptile House thrill children, with the Time Elevator plummeting the adults (virtually) through the history of the Island of Cyprus…

Places to Visit on Cyprus:

Kourion Ancient Site close to the City of Limassol

Although we have already visited here earlier in my book, Kourion, 18 km (12 miles) west of Limassol, is one of Cyprus's most impressive archaeological sites and well worth a second visit. Dating from the 12th century BC, this ancient settlement once looked majestically out over the Mediterranean. Highlights today include its amphitheatre, ruined Roman houses and mosaics. Visitors are sometimes lucky and can watch a concert in the ancient arena on a balmy summer's evening which is a hard-to-beat experience…

Places to Visit on Cyprus:

The Resort of Protaras

The resort with its year-round sunshine, warm climate and sandy beaches, it is easy to see why European holidaymaker's flock to Protaras every year. The eastern Cypriot resort also boasts a lengthy seaside promenade, perfect for a leisurely bicycle ride or sunset stroll, a myriad of restaurants, where alfresco dining is the norm, and a wealth of vibrant bars and clubs. For those who want to dip into the hedonistic nightlife of Ayia Napa, Cyprus's renowned party capital is just 16 km (10 miles) away. Whether you want to dance into the small hours of the morning, unwind on the beach, try your hand at watersports or treat the children to a day at the water park, Protaras is a resort that has something to offer everyone…

Places to Visit on Cyprus:

The Resort of Protaras

Protaras beach is called Fig Tree Bay by many and it is one of the best beaches on Cyprus's east coast. Its soft golden sand is the ideal place to spread out a towel and soak up the sun's rays before plunging into the warm and clear Mediterranean Sea. Opportunities for watersports abound, both at Fig Tree Bay and at the resort's other beaches…

Places to Visit on Cyprus:

The Resort of Protaras

When you stay in Protaras try to make a pilgrimage to the tiny Church of the Prophet Elias, which overlooks the resort from a 100 m-high hill. The 300-step ascent is rewarded with far reaching views of Protaras and the coast beyond. The vista is particularly impressive when the colourful spring flowers are in bloom. The beautiful Cavo Greko National Forest Park, with its myriad opportunities for cycling, horse riding and hiking is another must-see attraction nearby. Boat trips from Protaras provide a leisurely ideal vantage point from which to snap the pretty coast and the Cavo Greko sea caves…

Places to Visit on Cyprus:

The Resort of Protaras

Fringed by sandy beaches, some stretches of which are watched over by lifeguards, Protaras is an ideal resort for families. Restaurants are child-friendly, while watersports and the local water park provide more than enough activities to keep the children and even big kids happy for days…

Places to Visit on Cyprus:

The Kition Archaeological Site in Larnaca

Unearth Larnaca's ancient history at the Kition Archaeological Site or Ancient Kition, where excavations have revealed the site apparently dates back as far as the 13th century BC, before learning more about the oldest still-inhabited city in Cyprus by visiting its museums. Larnaca's 17th-century Turkish fort and the attractive orthodox St Lazurus Church also merit a visit…

Places to Visit on Cyprus:

Paphos Town

As we have already seen with its year-round sunshine, bath temperature seawater, sandy beaches and a relaxed ambience it is no surprise that the Cypriot resort of Paphos is booming. Throw in cooling sea breezes, some of the finest Greek relics and Roman mosaics anywhere in the world, relaxing spas, a lively nightlife scene, luxury hotels and decent restaurants make the myriad of its charms hard to resist. If that is not enough, many of Cyprus's stunning natural attractions, including Paphos Forest, the Akamas Peninsula and the Troodos Mountains, are close to the resort. When it comes to holidays, Paphos, with its sandy beaches, first-class resort facilities and UNESCO World Heritage-listed attractions, comes up trumps at any time of year and that is why we stayed there…

Places to Visit on Cyprus:

Paphos Town

In addition to the small stretches of often pebbly beach located next to the waterfront hotels of Kato Paphos, the resort also boasts the centrally located and sandy Municipal Beach. Faros Beach often proves a quieter option. Both of these beaches have been awarded EU blue flags for cleanliness. Another blue flag winner is Coral Bay, a lovely sandy beach 13 km (8 miles) north of Paphos that is easily accessible by local bus. Watersports operators located on the beach or operating from the resort hotels rent out everything from pedaloes to windsurfers...

Places to Visit on Cyprus:

Paphos Town

In Paphos Town there are ruins that date back to the 12th century BC, crumbing fortresses, ancient tombs and stunning Roman remnants which have all secured Paphos a place on the coveted UNESCO World Heritage list. Today the intricate mosaics of Nea Paphos, some of the most impressive in the world, and the voluminous Tombs of the Kings are amongst the resort's most popular attractions. The local Archaeological Museum sheds even more light on the centuries of intriguing history of the Town…

Places to Visit on Cyprus:

Paphos Town

Paphos Town is an ideal resort for families with it's sandy beaches, watersports, boat trips and a host of land based sporting activities including hiking in the Troodos Mountains and going on a Jeep Safari. The white-knuckle waterslides, wave pools and fast and lazy rivers at the Paphos Aphrodite Waterpark also await the visitor. It includes one of the biggest family rafting rides in Europe just the thing for the thrill seeking kids and the big kids alike…

Places to Visit on Cyprus:

The Troodos Mountains

Driving an hour northeast of Paphos Town brings you to the Troodos Mountains, a natural wonderland of hiking trails, lush forest and other indigenous fauna and flora; look out for wild sheep. Between November and March the area is blanketed in snow, with locals and holidaymakers taking advantage of the ski slopes and cross-country runs of the Troodos Ski Centre which is the most southerly in Europe. To the northwest of Paphos the Akamas peninsula is another great spot for a walk…

The Best Beaches on Cyprus

Coral Bay Beach

Rated as the best beach on the Western side of the Island of Cyprus. Coral Bay is a hit with both tourists and local villagers. It has classic golden sand that covers this spacious beach, where you will never struggle to find a peaceful spot for lazing under the sun. Crystal clear seawater that is safe for all to enjoy, and with a variety of watersports, family-friendly activities and various places to eat; Coral Bay offers something for everybody. The beach also has a number of stunning coves nearby, which offer exceptional diving opportunities…

The Best Beaches on Cyprus:

Fig Tree Bay Beach

Situated in the Protaras region of the Island, this popular beach has earned its name because of a lone Fig Tree which stands nearby. Legend has it the iconic tree was brought by invaders in the 17th century and has been there ever since, providing an eye-catching backdrop. Waves from the rich blue sea break gently onto the soft sands of the beach, which offers an exciting range of watersports for the thrill seekers, alongside calm seas for children to enjoy. A number of shops and cafes line the sands to suit all tastes, and if you want a break take a swim out to the small Island which sits just off the beach and soak up the breathtaking scenery on offer from there…

The Best Beaches on Cyprus:

Ladies Mile Beach - Limassol

Located on the edge of Limassol Town, Ladies Mile is one of the Towns best kept secrets. You can walk, often undisturbed, across the soft golden sand, taking in the natural beauty of this very special beach. Owing to its location the beach has a lack of natural shade, making it a firm favourite with sun worshipers. If it all gets too much though, one of the best ways to cool off is by taking a dip in the crystal clear seawater which provide safe swimming conditions for everyone to enjoy. It is this calm sea which attracts a number of daring windsurfers to the beach each year, which also has plenty of other watersports on offer for your entertainment…

The Best Beaches on Cyprus:

Nissi Beach

Found in the Cypriot party capital of Ayia Napa, Nissi Beach is regarded, by many, as one of the best all-round beaches on the Island. It has iconic white sand which sweep across the bay which can prove irresistible as they gleam under the sun, whilst the tranquil blue seawater is the ideal way to cool off. Entertainment is provided throughout the day with a selection of bars and cafes available to suit your mood, whether you are looking to take a break or continue to soak up the party atmosphere. There's also an exciting range of watersports to test yourself out in the waves, or bungee jumps should you feel brave enough! If all that seems too much though, why not have a swim out from the beach towards the beaches own Desert Island, from where you can really take in the true beauty of this holiday paradise…

The Best Beaches on Cyprus:

Pissouri Beach

The beach can be found tucked away in the sleepy resort of Pissouri. It has soft sand and the crystal clear seawater in the untouched bay are difficult to resist, and a peaceful atmosphere is ensured thanks to the beach having wide open spaces. The beach is popular with people who enjoy water sports and there is a good range of activities to choose from. If you want to explore the coastline you can hire a pedaloes or crash across the waves using a jet-ski. If you need a break from the beach, there is a number of good tavernas that line the beach at Pissouri, offering you the chance to try some of the delicious freshly cooked local dishes…

The Best Beaches on Cyprus:

Perbola Beach

Located on the eastern side of Limassol Town, the east part of the 730 m long beach is sandy and the west is rocky. On the coastal part of the beach there are some tavernas. In the seawater two underwater breakwaters have been built that help protect the seafront from the strong waves that sometimes hits the shore here…

The Best Beaches on Cyprus:

Avdimou Beach

The beach is located in Avdimou Village in the Limassol District. It is a wide and sandy beach that is safe for children as the seawater level is relatively shallow. Close by there are some tavernas and bars. Avdimou village is located on the west of Limassol towards the town of Paphos. It is mainly an agricultural community with emphasis on wine production from its grape plantations…

The Best Beaches on Cyprus:

Alykes Beach

Alykes is a good sandy beach situated near the hotels in the tourist area known as Kato Paphos. There is a bus stop nearby and access to the beach is easy and well sign-posted. The quality of the seawater is tested frequently and the beachfront is cleaned every day. Water sports, sun bed and umbrella hire are available on the beach. Lifeguards are on duty with lifesaving equipment in the summer season. The beach is accessible by walking, bus, car, motorbike and bicycle. Accommodation facilities are available nearby…

The Best Beaches on Cyprus:

Faros Beach

Faros beach is a sandy beach situated at the western end of Paphos Town. Access to the beach is easy and well sign-posted. The quality of the seawater is tested frequently and the beach front is cleaned every day. Water sports, sun bed and umbrella hire are available from April to October. Lifeguards are on duty with lifesaving equipment during the same months. There is also a beach volleyball court. The beach is accessible by bus, car, motorbike, bicycle or even on foot…

The Best Beaches on Cyprus:

Geroskipou Municipal Beach

The beach is located in the village of Geroskipou. This sandy beach is easily reached by car, motorbike, bicycle and bus. Water sports, sun bed and umbrella hire are available on the beach. There are accommodation facilities nearby while lifeguards are usually on duty with lifesaving equipment during the summer season…

The Best Beaches on Cyprus:

Laourou Beach Pegeia

The beach is located in the village of Pegeia. This sandy beach is easily reached by car, motorbike, bicycle and bus. Water sports, sun bed and umbrella hire are available on the beach. There are accommodation facilities nearby while lifeguards are usually on duty with lifesaving equipment during the summer season…

The Best Beaches on Cyprus:

Paphos Municipal Baths Beach

This beach is a favourite with the locals, Municipal Baths Beach is a sandy beach with very few rocks. It is located in the heart of the tourist area of Kato Paphos and 300 metres from Paphos Castle. Access to the beach is easy and there are signs with directions showing the way to the facilities. Water sports, sun bed and umbrella hire are available on site from April to October. Lifeguards are usually on duty with lifesaving equipment during the summer period. There are numerous good quality restaurants, tavernas, bars and lots of accommodation facilities located nearby…

The Best Beaches on Cyprus:

Polis Chrysochous Municipal Beach

The beach is located in the village of Polis Chrysochous. It is a sandy beach mixed with pebbles and is easily reached by car, motorbike and bus. Water sports, sun bed and umbrella hire are available on the beach. There are accommodation facilities nearby while lifeguards are usually on duty with lifesaving equipment during the summer season…

The Best Beaches on Cyprus:

Pachyammos Bay Beach in Paphos

Pachyammos Bay has a narrow sandy beach with very few rocks. It is situated in the Paphos tourist area, in front of the hotels. Well sign-posted, the beach is accessible by walking, bus, car, motorbike and bicycle. Water sports, sun beds and umbrellas are available from June to October. Accommodation facilities, bars, restaurants and telephones can be found nearby. The quality of the seawater is tested frequently and the beachfront is cleaned daily. Lifeguards are usually on duty with lifesaving equipment during the summer season…

The Holiday Voyage

Susie and Alan on Holiday…

When we were on holiday on Cyprus we went on a five day tour to explore the rich history of the Holy Land and that of ancient Egypt. Our ship left the Port of Limassol one early evening and steamed off into the sunset. On the boat we had our own cabin and all meals and entertainment were provided throughout our trip both on land and at sea. Every visit, on land was led by an expert guide so we received plenty of useful information about the places we were going to visit each day. Our first port of call was Israel (the Holy Land)…

The Holiday Voyage:

The City of Jerusalem

Located in the Judean Mountains between the Mediterranean Sea and the Dead Sea, the City of Jerusalem is considered holy to the three major Abrahamic religions of Judaism, Christianity, and Islam. It is the holiest city in Judaism and the spiritual centre of the Jewish people since the 10th century BC, the City is the third-holiest in Islam. The City is home to a number of significant and ancient Christian landmarks. It is also a city with a very violent past, as it has been fiercely contested between Christianity and Islam during the brutal Crusade era and since. Although the city has had a large Jewish majority population since 1967, a wide range of national, religious, and socioeconomic groups are represented here…

The Holiday Voyage:

The City of Jerusalem

The walled area of Jerusalem, which until the late nineteenth century formed the entire city, is now called the Old City and became a UNESCO World Heritage Site in 1982. It consists of four ethnic and religious sections which are the Armenian, Christian, Jewish, and Muslim Quarters. The Old City is home to several of Jerusalem's most important and contested religious sites including the Western Wall and Temple Mount for Jews, the Dome of the Rock and al-Aqsa Mosque for Muslims, and the Church of the Holy Sepulchre for Christians. We spent a morning walking around the narrow streets, we visited the walling wall and the Holy Sepulchre Church and several other famous ancient sites before boarding the coach to go onto the City of Bethlehem …

The Holiday Voyage:

The City of Bethlehem in the Holy Land

The City of Bethlehem is the Birthplace of Jesus and is therefore, the Cradle of Christianity. Located about six miles southwest of Jerusalem, Bethlehem is a City of approximately 30,000 inhabitants, half of whom are Muslims and half of whom are Christians. Bethlehem is best known for being the birthplace of Jesus Christ, but it is also sacred to Muslims and Jews. The Church of the Nativity in Manger Square, one of the most important Israel travel destinations for Christians, is located in Bethlehem. Christian pilgrims have walked from Jerusalem to Manger Square for centuries. We visited the Church of the Nativity in Manger Square and found our time there inspiring and uplifting …

The Holiday Voyage:

The City of Bethlehem

The Church of the Nativity, the oldest church in the Holy Land, was founded by Constantine and his mother St. Helene in 326 A.D. The church was built over the Grotto of the Nativity, where Jesus Christ was born. The manger is located on the north side of the Grotto and an altar dedicated to the wise men is situated across from the manger. We joined our companions in visiting the Grotto and marvelled at the beauty of the shine that is now erected on the spot of the birth of Jesus…

The Holiday Voyage:

The Shrine in the City of Bethlehem

After visiting the church we joined the throng in Manger Square which is Bethlehem's pedestrian-only central plaza, where vibrant Christmas Eve festivities take place each year. Manger Square is surrounded by the Church of the Nativity, the Church of St. Catherine, the Palestinian Peace Centre, and the Mosque of Omar. We then had lunch in a local hotel before going onto the Milk Grotto…

The Holiday Voyage:

Bethlehem

Our last visit of the day was to the Milk Grotto which is where Mary, Joseph, and baby Jesus took shelter to hide from Herod's soldiers during the Slaughter of the Innocents. It is said that Mary nursed Jesus there before heading to Egypt. According to tradition, her milk fell to the floor of the cave, causing the rock to transform into white, chalky stone. Lactating mothers believe that the Milk Grotto has healing powers. After the visit we returned to our ship ready to leave Israel. Once onboard it was up anchor and off to visit the land of the Pharaoh's Egypt…

The Holiday Voyage:

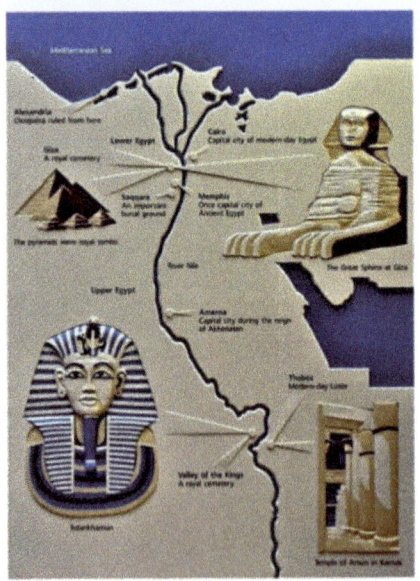

Port Said in Egypt

Port Said is a City that lies in the north east of Egypt which extends about 30 kilometres (19 miles) along the coast of the Mediterranean Sea, north of the Suez Canal, with an approximate population of 603,787 (2010). The City was established in 1859 during the building of the Suez Canal…

The Holiday Voyage:

Port Said in Egypt

Port Said is ranked the second largest amongst Egyptian cities after Cairo. The economic base of the city is fishing and industries, like chemicals, processed food, and cigarettes. Port Said is also an important harbour for exports of Egyptian products like cotton and rice, but also a re-fuelling station for ships that pass through the Suez Canal. It thrives on being a duty-free port, as well as a tourist resort especially during the summer months. It is home to the Lighthouse of Port Said (the first building in the world to be built from reinforced concrete)…

The Holiday Voyage:

Port Said in Egypt

In Port Said there are numerous old houses with grand balconies on all floors, giving the city a distinctive look. Port Said's twin city is Port Fuad, which lies on the eastern bank of the Suez Canal. The two cities coexist, to the extent that there is hardly any town centre in Port Fuad. The cities are connected by free ferries running all through the day, and together they form a metropolitan area with over a million residents that extends both on the African and the Asian sides of the Suez Canal. The only other metropolitan area in the world that also spans two continents is the City of Istanbul in Turkey…

The Holiday Voyage:

Port Said in Egypt

Port Said has been a global city since it was established and flourished particularly during the nineteenth and the first half of the twentieth century when it was inhabited by various nationalities and religions. Most of them were from Mediterranean countries, and they coexisted in tolerance, forming a friendly cosmopolitan community. When our ship arrived at the port it was time for us all to disembark onto coaches. Once the coach was full we left the port and travelled through the Egyptian countryside making our way, with great excitement, to the Giza plateau to see all of its ancient wonders…

The Holiday Voyage:

The Giza Plateau Egypt

The Giza Plateau is located west and south of the modern City of Cairo, in the vast desert that was imagined by the ancient Egyptians to be the land of the dead. Guarded by the Great Sphinx, the plateau is dominated by the massive pyramids of Khufu (Cheops), Khafre (Chephren), and Menkaure (Mycerinus), all of whom ruled Egypt during the 4th Dynasty (c. 2500 BC). The Royal pyramid complexes, which include temples, causeways, and satellite pyramids, are surrounded by tombs of the elite-members of the royal family, the nobility, and the priesthood. At the foot of the plateau, south of the Great Sphinx, lie the Cemetery and Town of the Pyramid Builders, where the men and women who designed and constructed the Royal and elite tombs on the main plateau lived, worked, died and were buried…

The Holiday Voyage:

The Giza Plateau Egypt

When we arrived just below the Giza Plateau we all trooped off the coach and into a camel stable to get mounted up on these surly beasts and then make our way up onto the plateau. I loved my camel ride and felt such joy in arriving at the Great Pyramid on the back of such a noble beast just like the Pharaohs may have done in the distant past. The Giza Plateau is probably the most famous site in Egypt, Giza has fascinated people for millennia. Although the archaeological and historical evidence proves without a doubt that the Great Pyramid of Khufu and its companions are Royal tombs built during the Old Kingdom, alternative theorists continue to argue that they were built by aliens or people from the mythical land of Atlantis. The pyramids are indeed remarkable feats of engineering. The Great Pyramid is aligned to the cardinal directions to within 1 degree of arc. However, this was within the engineering capabilities of Egypt's early Kings, and there is no need to create outlandish theories to explain its construction. The pyramids were built in fact by very skilled, talented and hard working Egyptians…

The Holiday Voyage:

The Giza Plateau Egypt

The Giza Plateau remained an important religious and Royal site right through the New Kingdom and Third Intermediate Period, and on into the Late Period of the Pharaohs. Significant monuments from these later eras include a New Kingdom temple to the Sphinx and a Temple of Isis which is an expansion of the mortuary chapel of one of the queens' pyramids next to the Great Pyramid…

The Holiday Voyage:

The Great Pyramid of Giza Egypt

The Great Pyramid of Giza which is also known as the Pyramid of Khufu or the Pyramid of Cheops is the oldest and largest of the three pyramids on the Gaza Pyramid complex bordering what is now El Giza, Egypt. The Great Pyramid of Giza is the oldest of the Seven Wonders of the Ancient World, and the only one to remain largely intact. Based on a mark in an interior chamber naming a work gang and a reference to fourth dynasty Egyptian Pharaoh Khufu Egyptologists believe that the pyramid was built as a tomb over a 10 to 20-year period by about 25,000 skilled workers (some may have been slaves) who concluded the building work in about 2560 BC. Initially at 146.5 metres (481 feet), the Great Pyramid was the tallest man-made structure in the world for more than 3,800 years…

The Holiday Voyage:

The Great Pyramid of Giza Egypt

Originally, the Great Pyramid was covered by casing stones that formed a smooth outer surface; what is seen today is the underlying core structure. Some of the casing stones that once covered the structure can still be seen scattered around the base. There have been varying scientific and alternative theories about the Great Pyramid's construction techniques. The most accepted construction hypotheses is based on the idea that it was built by moving huge stones from a quarry, dragging and then lifting them into place manually...

The Holiday Voyage:

The Great Pyramid of Giza Egypt

There are three known chambers inside the Great Pyramid. The lowest chamber is cut into the bedrock upon which the pyramid was built and was left unfinished. The others are the Queen's Chamber and the King's Chamber which are higher up within the pyramid structure. To my great delight and joy I ventured inside the pyramid entrance and explored the chambers. Whilst there you could really sense the power and majesty of this wonderful building. It made you realise the vastness of the construction and its history and to be actually walking inside the pyramid made me feel that in fact I was actually back in time and part of its history. It was not just magnificent it was mammoth! The main part of the Giza complex is a set of buildings that included two mortuary temples in honour of Khufu (one close to the pyramid and one near the Nile), three smaller pyramids for Khufu's wives, an even smaller "satellite" pyramid, a raised causeway connecting the two temples, and small mataba tombs surrounding the pyramid for Egyptian nobles…

The Holiday Voyage:

The Sphinx of Egypt

Having visited the Great Pyramid and venturing inside it was now time for us all to trooped down the hill in the blazing sun to marvel at the truly majestic Sphinx. The Sphinx is on the edge of the Giza Plateau, near the City of Cairo, Egypt. As you walk towards it you experience the feeling that you are in the presence of the greatest monumental sculpture ever built in the ancient world. The Sphinx is carved out of a single ridge of stone 240 feet (73 meters) long and 66 feet (20 meters) high. The head of the Sphinx, which has a markedly different texture from the body, and shows far less severe erosion, is a naturally occurring outcrop of harder stone. To form the lower body of the Sphinx, enormous blocks of stone were quarried from the base rock (and these blocks were then used in the core masonry of the temples directly in front and to the south of the Sphinx)…

The Holiday Voyage:

The Sphinx of Egypt

I was very interested to learn that while a few stubborn Egyptologists still maintain that the Sphinx was constructed in the 4th Dynasty by the Pharaoh Chephren (Khafre). An accumulating body of evidence, both archaeological and geological, indicates that the Sphinx is far older than the 4th Dynasty, and was only restored by Chephren during his reign. There are no inscriptions on the Sphinx, or on any of the temples connected to it that, offer evidence of its construction by Chephren, yet the so-called 'Inventory Stele' (uncovered on the Giza plateau in the 19th century) tells that the Pharaoh Cheops who reigned before Chephren ordered a temple built alongside the Sphinx, meaning of course that the Sphinx was already there, and thus could not have been constructed by Chephren…

The Holiday Voyage:

The Sphinx of Egypt

A much greater age for the Sphinx has been suggested and recent geologists have confirmed, that the extreme erosion on the body of the Sphinx could not be the result of wind and sand, as has been universally assumed, but rather was the result of water action. Geologists agree that in the distant past Egypt was subjected to severe flooding. Wind erosion cannot take place when the body of the Sphinx is covered by sand, and the Sphinx has been in this condition for nearly all of the last five thousand years and certainly since the alleged time of its 4th Dynasty construction…

The Holiday Voyage:

The Sphinx of Egypt

If wind-blown sand had indeed caused the deep erosion of the Sphinx, we would expect to find evidence of such erosion on other Egyptian monuments built of similar materials and exposed to the wind for a similar length of time. Yet the fact of the matter is, that even on structures that have had more exposure to the wind-blown sand, there are minimal effects of erosion evident, the sand having done little more than scour clean the surface of the dressed stones…

The Holiday Voyage:

The Sphinx of Egypt

Additional evidence for the great age of the Sphinx may perhaps be indicated by the astronomical significance of its shape, being that of a lion. Roughly every two thousand years (2160 to be exact), and because of the precession of the equinoxes, the sun on the vernal equinox rises against the stellar background of a different constellation. For the past two thousand years that constellation has been Pisces the Fish, symbol of the Christian age. Prior to the age of Pisces it was the age of Aries the Ram, and before that it was the age of Taurus the Bull…

The Holiday Voyage:

Rameses The Great…

The Sphinx of Egypt

It is interesting to note that during the first and second millennia BC, approximately the Age of Aries, ram-oriented iconography was common in Dynastic Egypt, while during the Age of Taurus the Bull-cult arose in Minoan Crete. Perhaps the builders of the Sphinx likewise used astrological symbolism in designing their monumental sculpture. The geological findings discussed above indicate that the Sphinx seems to have been sculpted sometime before 10,000 BC, and this period coincides with the Age of Leo the Lion, which lasted from 10,970 to 8810 BC. Now that we have established these facts it was time, with great regret, to leave the Sphinx and board the coach, once more, and head further down the hill into the vibrant City of Cairo…

The Holiday Voyage:

The City of Cairo

Cairo is the capital and largest City in Egypt. Greater Cairo is the largest metropolitan area in the Middle East and the Arab World and the 15th largest in the World. It is strongly linked with ancient Egypt, as the World famous Giza Pyramid Complex and the ancient City of Memphis are located nearby. The City is located near the River Nile Delta. The modern City of Cairo was founded in 969 AD but the land composing of the present-day City was the site of the ancient national capital whose remnants remain visible in parts of Old City of Cairo today…

The Holiday Voyage:

The Old Bazaar
In Cairo…

The City of Cairo

The City of Cairo is like many other large Cities in that it suffers from high levels of pollution, traffic noise and congestion. Cairo's metro is one of only two metros on the African continent. The other City with a metro is in Algiers. The Cairo metro is amongst the fifteen busiest in the world, with over 1 billion annual passenger rides. The economy of Cairo was ranked first in the Middle East in 2005, and 43 rd globally. After spending some time looking at all the sights and sounds of the City and making the obligatory visit to **The Old Bazaar in Cairo!** Shopping done it was all back onto the coach and with great excitement it was now time for us to go and see the **Greatest Show on Earth**…

The Holiday Voyage:

The Cairo Egyptian Museum (The Greatest Show on Earth)

As the coach pulled up outside of the Cairo Egyptian Museum I could not have been any more excited because this building houses real ancient treasure. In the past I had read lots and seen much (TV, DVD's and Films) about the Ancient Egyptians, The Valley of the Kings, the greatest pharaoh of them all Rameses II, the boy King Tutankhamun and all of the **Wonderful Things** that Howard Carter had found in his tomb. **TODAY** I was going to see them all with my own eyes. So today I would have been inside the Great Pyramid, seen the Sphinx, visited an old bazaar in Cairo and now it was time to marvel at Rameses II, the boy King Tutankhamun and all of the other wonderful things inside the Cairo Museum. Oh how lucky was I and so I entered the museum with wide eyes and great joy…

The Holiday Voyage:

The Cairo Egyptian Museum (The Greatest Show on Earth)

The Museum of Egyptian Antiquities, known commonly as the Egyptian Museum or Museum of Cairo, in the City of Cairo, Egypt, is home to an extensive collection of ancient Egyptian antiquities. It has about 120,000 items, with a representative number on public display, the remainder are held in storerooms. There are two main floors in the museum, the ground floor and the first floor. On the ground floor there is an extensive collection of papyrus and coins that were used in the Ancient World. The numerous pieces of papyrus are generally small fragments, due to their decay over the past two millennia. Several languages are found on these pieces, including Greek, Latin, Arabic, and ancient Egyptian. The coins found on this floor are made of many different metals, including gold, silver, and bronze. The coins are not only Egyptian, but also Greek, Roman, and Islamic. This has helped historians to research the history of Ancient Egyptian trade. Also on the ground floor are artifacts from the New Kingdom, the time period between 1550 and 1069 BC. These artifacts are generally larger than items created in earlier centuries. Those items include statues, tables, and coffins (sarcophagi). On the first floor there are artifacts from the final two dynasties of Egypt, including items from the tombs of the Pharaohs Thutmosis III, Thutmosis IV, Amenophis II, Hatshepsut, and the courtier Maiherpri, as well as many artifacts from the Valley of the Kings, in particular the material from the intact tombs of Tutankhamun and Psusennes I. Two special rooms contain a number of mummies of Kings and other Royal family members of the New Kingdom…

The Holiday Voyage:

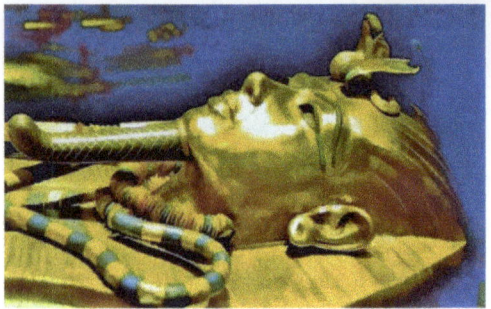

Tutankhamun and Rameses II

The Cairo Egyptian Museum (The Greatest Show on Earth)

As I stepped inside the famous museum the first thing I saw was an enormous statue of my favourite pharaoh Rameses II (see above). Ramesses II, also known as Ramesses the Great, was the third pharaoh of the Nineteenth Dynasty of Egypt. He is often regarded as the greatest, most celebrated, and most powerful pharaoh of the Egyptian Empire. His successors and later Egyptians called him the "Great Ancestor". Ramesses II led several military expeditions into the Levant, reasserting Egyptian control over Canaan. He also led expeditions to the south, into Nubia, commemorated in inscriptions at Beit el-Wali and Gerf Hussein. Having marveled at the imposing statue, for some time, I wandered around, looking at all of the ancient treasures on show. I, like everyone else soon found myself in front of the golden death mask of Tutankhamun. Words cannot do this mask justice so I hope that the picture above gives you some idea of the majesty of this incredible artifact. As I stood there amazed at what I was seeing the guide told us that Tutankhamun was an Egyptian pharaoh of the 18th dynasty, during the period of Egyptian history known as the New Kingdom or sometimes the New Empire Period. He has since his discovery been colloquially referred to as King Tut. His original name, Tutankhaten, means "Living Image of Aten", while Tutankhamun means "Living Image of Amun". In hieroglyphs, the name Tutankhamun was typically written Amen-tut-ankh, because of a scribal custom that placed a divine name at the beginning of a phrase to show appropriate reverence...

The Holiday Voyage:

The Cairo Egyptian Museum (The Greatest Show on Earth)

In the Cairo Museum you will see many of the mummies of the most powerful people in ancient Egypt - the Pharaohs. Pharaoh is the common title of the monarchs of ancient Egypt from the First Dynasty until the Macedonian conquest in 305 BC, although the actual term "Pharaoh" was not used contemporaneously for a ruler until circa 1200 BC. In antiquity the pharaoh was the political and religious leader of the Egyptian people, holding the titles: 'Lord of the Two Lands' and 'High Priest of Every Temple'…

The Holiday Voyage:

The Cairo Egyptian Museum (The Greatest Show on Earth)

The Pharaoh as 'Lord of the Two Lands' was the ruler of Upper and Lower Egypt. He was ruler and owner of all of the land of Egypt, he made the laws, collected the taxes, and defended Egypt against its enemies. As 'High Priest of Every Temple', the pharaoh represented the gods on Earth. He performed rituals and built temples to honour those gods. Many pharaohs actually went to war when their land was threatened or when they wanted to control foreign lands. If the pharaoh won the battle, the conquered people had to recognise the Egyptian pharaoh as their ruler and offer him the finest and most valuable goods as tributes from their land. So with all this information going around in our heads we reluctantly trudged down the steps out of the Cairo Egyptian Museum. As the sun set over Cairo, the Sphinx and the Pyramids of Giza it was back on the coach, then onto the ship, and back to the Paradise Island of Cyprus to continue our sun, sand and sea holiday. We were all very tired but I personally felt so much richer for all that I had seen and learnt during the last five wonderful days. As the ship sailed out into the blue Mediterranean Sea I reflected on our visit to the Holy Land and the Land of the Pharaohs and concluded that this journey of discovery was one of the greatest experiences of my life. Just before we complete our journey there is just time, in the last chapter, to enjoy the Island of Cyprus in Colour …

Cyprus in Colour

The Paradise Island of Cyprus…

Cyprus in Colour:

The Paradise Island of Cyprus…

Cyprus in Colour:

The Paradise Island of Cyprus…

Cyprus in Colour:

The Paradise Island of Cyprus…

Cyprus in Colour:

The Paradise Island of Cyprus…

Cyprus in Colour:

The Paradise Island of Cyprus…

Cyprus in Colour:

The Paradise Island of Cyprus…

Cyprus in Colour:

The Paradise Island of Cyprus…

Cyprus in Colour:

The Paradise Island of Cyprus…

Cyprus in Colour:

The Paradise Island of Cyprus…

Cyprus in Colour:

The Paradise Island of Cyprus…

Cyprus in Colour:

The Paradise Island of Cyprus…

Cyprus in Colour:

The Paradise Island of Cyprus…

Cyprus in Colour:

The Paradise Island of Cyprus…

Cyprus in Colour:

The Paradise Island of Cyprus…

Cyprus in Colour:

The Paradise Island of Cyprus…

Cyprus in Colour:

The Paradise Island of Cyprus…

Cyprus in Colour:

The Paradise Island of Cyprus…

Cyprus in Colour:

The Paradise Island of Cyprus…

Cyprus in Colour:

The Paradise Island of Cyprus…

Cyprus in Colour:

The Paradise Island of Cyprus…

Cyprus in Colour:

The Paradise Island of Cyprus…

Cyprus in Colour:

The Paradise Island of Cyprus…

Cyprus in Colour:

The Paradise Island of Cyprus…

Cyprus in Colour:

The Paradise Island of Cyprus…

Cyprus in Colour:

The Paradise Island of Cyprus…

Cyprus in Colour:

The Paradise Island of Cyprus…

Cyprus in Colour:

The Paradise Island of Cyprus…

Cyprus in Colour:

The Paradise Island of Cyprus…

Cyprus in Colour:

The Paradise Island of Cyprus…

Cyprus in Colour:

The Paradise Island of Cyprus…

Cyprus in Colour:

The Paradise Island of Cyprus…

Cyprus in Colour:

The Paradise Island of Cyprus…

Cyprus in Colour:

The Paradise Island of Cyprus…

Cyprus in Colour:

The Paradise Island of Cyprus…

Cyprus in Colour:

The Paradise Island of Cyprus…

Cyprus in Colour:

The Paradise Island of Cyprus…

Cyprus in Colour:

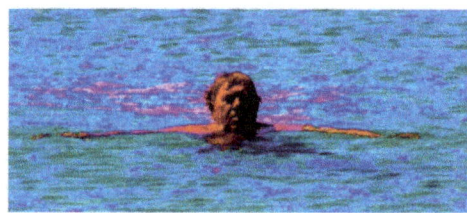

The Paradise Island of Cyprus…

Cyprus in Colour:

The Paradise Island of Cyprus…

Cyprus in Colour:

The Paradise Island of Cyprus…

Cyprus in Colour:

The Paradise Island of Cyprus…

Cyprus in Colour:

The Paradise Island of Cyprus…

Cyprus in Colour:

The Paradise Island of Cyprus…

Cyprus in Colour:

The Paradise Island of Cyprus…

Cyprus in Colour:

The Paradise Island of Cyprus…

Cyprus in Colour:

The Paradise Island of Cyprus…

Cyprus in Colour:

The Paradise Island of Cyprus…

Cyprus in Colour:

The Paradise Island of Cyprus…

Cyprus in Colour:

As we come to the end of our journey to the paradise Island of Cyprus, the Holy Land and the Land of the Pharaohs it just leaves me time to thank you for coming on this voyage of discovery with me. I hope that you have enjoyed our time together and so until the next time goodbye and happy holidays…

Acknowledgement

I would like to thank all the people of Cyprus, Israel and Egypt that we met during our holiday on their beautiful Island, the Holy Land and at the Giza Pyramids, Cairo Museum and especially a big thank you to our tour guide Lizzy. I would also like to thank my publishers Rainbow Publications UK. For publishing this book and for giving me the opportunity for my book to be read. Finally I wish to thank my wife Susie for all the love and support that she gives me in all that I do every day of my life.

Susie… 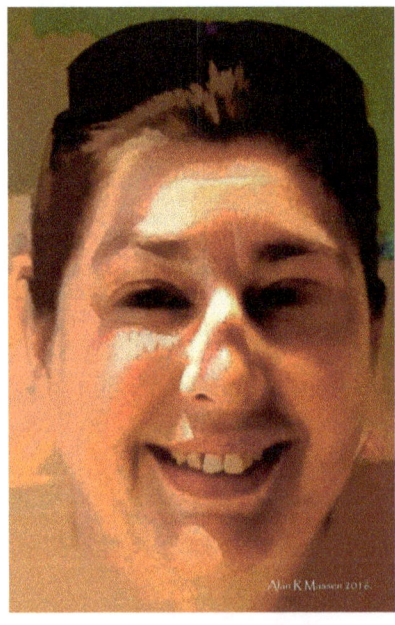  …Alan

Copyright © 2019 Alan R. Massen

I would like to wish them all a very big

Thank You

www.ingramcontent.com/pod-product-compliance
Lightning Source LLC
Chambersburg PA
CBHW061926290426
44113CB00024B/2831